PERSONAL POWER
THROUGH THE
SPIRITUAL
DISCIPLINES

PERSONAL POWER
THROUGH THE
SPIRITUAL
DISCIPLINES

G. Ernest Thomas

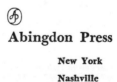

Abingdon Press

New York
Nashville

PERSONAL POWER THROUGH THE SPIRITUAL DISCIPLINES

Copyright © 1960 by Abingdon Press

240
+ ho

Library of Congress Catalog Card Number: 60-12074

SET UP, PRINTED, AND BOUND BY THE
PARTHENON PRESS, AT NASHVILLE,
TENNESSEE, UNITED STATES OF AMERICA

For
CAROL ANN THOMAS

my beloved daughter

Personal power must be earned
by each new generation
through spiritual discipline

PREFACE

A man or woman can be only a nominal Christian without being criticized. Social standing is not threatened if church membership signifies no more than a name which appears on the rolls. But something is lost to the church when interest is merely casual, and even more is sacrificed by the individual himself. The Christian faith is a source of personal power when it springs from a close relationship between a man and his God.

Vital Christianity exacts a price. It requires the disciplines which have their source in the teachings of Jesus. When these practices shape the devotional life and conduct of Christians we lay claim to an endless source of spiritual strength.

Discipline implies self-control. It suggests struggle against forces which tend to ridicule or disregard a wise course of action. The disciplines of the spiritual life have to be maintained even in those moments when the hectic pressures of the world almost persuade us that we have no time for God.

Making a place each day for worship, Bible

reading, prayer, service, witnessing, and the other disciplines will be a struggle until they become fixed habits. Only when this has been achieved can we overcome the demands of selfish and worldly interests.

This book deals with the spiritual disciplines. It is designed primarily to be used for personal meditation or for family devotions. It will also provide guidance for the numerous prayer and fellowship groups which are searching for keys to spiritual power. The chapters may be the subject for individual study and for discussion in weekly meetings.

I am indebted to many persons for the ideas presented in these chapters. Ralph S. Cushman introduced me to the devotional habits, and his writings have shaped my personal thinking and my devotional practices. My wife is a companion in spiritual adventures, as well as a source of continued encouragement. Mrs. Ralph F. Worthy, my secretary, is always helpful and patient as I struggle to give form to ideas. For these, and many others who are unnamed, I am grateful.

G. ERNEST THOMAS

CONTENTS

9

CONTENTS

THE DISCIPLINE
OF WORSHIP

1st Day

THE FOUNDATION FOR WORSHIP

By whom also we have access [to God] by faith.
—Rom. 5:2

H. G. Wells told of a businessman who lived under such strain that he was in serious danger of a mental breakdown. His doctor advised him to seek for the peace which fellowship with God could give him. "What!" he exclaimed, "to think of that, up there, having fellowship with me! I would as soon think of cooling my throat with the milky way or shaking hands with the stars!"

Many people are unable to conceive that God is available to be known and worshiped. Some Christians find it difficult to think that the God who created the vast universe is a being whom they can know. They may desperately need the strength and power which God can give, but they cannot understand why the Creator should be aware of them.

Millions of Christians have found the answer to this problem in God's revelation of himself in Jesus. We worship the Father whose nature was made known in the man of Nazareth. We find the key to the problems of the universe in the one who walked the Galilean road. Eternal time and space are brought within our comprehension.

No writer in the Bible understood the mission of Christ better than did the author of Hebrews. The entire book is designed to make it clear that a full and supreme revelation of God has come to men through Jesus Christ.

Throughout the ages Christians have ended their prayers with the words "through Jesus Christ our Lord." Often he has been called the "mediator." The Christian faith rests upon our confidence that the work of Jesus was much more than that of a teacher or example. In a way that is true of the founder of no other religion, Jesus is the bridge-builder between man and God. In his life we see and understand the attributes of the heavenly Father. In his continuing work we are able to seek and to know God. Jesus is the high priest who makes worship not merely rites and ceremonies to appease an angry deity, but an act of intimate fellowship with a loving Father.

Christians regularly observe the discipline of public worship. In such moments our thoughts center upon Jesus Christ. By knowledge of him we have access through faith to the grace of God. When we go to church with expectant hearts we learn how better to understand both the universe and ourselves.

PRAYER

We thank thee, O God, for the revelation of thyself in Christ. Forgive us if we lose thee in the universe because our thoughts have not been centered upon Christ. Help us to walk with him this day, and in his fellowship may we find ourselves with thee. *Amen.*

Read Rom. 5:1-5

2nd Day

WORSHIP AND THE PRESENCE

> *Falling on his face, he will worship God and declare that God is really among you.*
>
> —I COR. 14:25 (R.S.V.)

The final test of any act of public or private worship is whether it helps us to know and to feel the presence of God. Joseph Twitchell told of a visit to the home of Horace Bushnell when Bushnell was an old man. They had walked together in the early evening out on a hillside. As the darkness came Bushnell said, "Let us kneel and pray." Then Bushnell lifted his voice to God. When he told about the incident later, Twitchell said, "I was afraid to stretch out my hand in the darkness in case I should touch God."

Often our worship fails to reach that high goal. In spite of rituals, or prayers, or readings, God still seems far away. Yet we recognize that the failure to feel intimate contact with him is not God's choice. He is ready and willing to be close to those who seek him.

15

The Letter to the Hebrews must have stirred memories in Jewish minds of the beautiful ceremonies by which men sought on the Day of Atonement to claim the mercy of God. It was the season when all things and all people were cleansed and sin was wiped out. The worship was accompanied by elaborate rituals conducted by the high priest. The robes worn were colorful; and incense and special lamps were an important part of the setting. The entire ceremony was beautiful.

We, too, are grateful for beauty in our services of worship. Church spires which point to the sky and sanctuaries which are illumined by stained-glass windows inspire reverence. Robed choirs and candles have their place in creating a spirit which makes worldly interests and desires seem less important.

We need beauty in worship: our spirits are hushed and our desires purified by the Christian symbols of holiness. But we must not lose sight of the eternal certainty that God is available at all times as a living presence to those who seek him. Through faith the way is opened wherever we may be, or whatever may be the surroundings.

Sometimes it is the spirit with which we approach an hour of worship that shuts God out. We cannot mechanically go through the motions of devotion and expect to achieve an awareness of his presence. Rituals in themselves have no magic to force God's attention. True worship demands penitence on the part of the seeker and complete surrender to the will of the heavenly Father.

Whenever we feel as near to God as to the person who

kneels beside us we know that we have experienced an act of true worship.

PRAYER

Dear heavenly Father, we want to know thee better. We yearn for the consciousness of thy presence—unworthy as we are. Come and bless this moment of seeking. Give us the joy of true worship. In Jesus' name. *Amen.*

Read I Cor. 14:23-25

3rd Day

THE HABIT OF WORSHIP

> *Not forsaking the assembling of ourselves together.*
>
> —Heb. 10:25

Regular attendance at services of worship is the first and simplest duty of anyone who says that he believes in Christ. Faith begins to die on the Sunday when a Christian decides: "I guess I won't go to church today."

When attendance at services becomes an established discipline in our daily lives, we discover an endless source of personal power. William Gladstone said to a colleague in the British government: "I would no more think of missing church on Sunday than I would of missing my breakfast." The discipline had become deeply fixed in his life. He was

17

able to bear the heavy responsibilities of the prime minister's office because he found a fresh supply of power as he worshiped with others in God's house.

Many of the questions which arise concerning the practice of going to church will be avoided if we make it a fixed habit. A businessman remarked to a group of friends that he wondered sometimes if his family were peculiar. "I have never had difficulty getting my children to go to church," he said. "From the time they were able to walk we have taken them to church school and morning service. They must like it, for they never have mentioned any wish to stay home." He didn't realize it, but his family demonstrates what it means to have a set discipline. It is inevitable that many families face resistance if each Sunday brings renewed discussion as to whether or not parents and children will attend church.

It should not be necessary for us to scan the skies on Sunday morning before deciding whether or not we will go to church—God is at work in the world when it rains as well as when the sun is shining. In many parts of the earth there is added reason for thanks to God when it is raining. It should not be necessary for us to inquire of our guests whether they want to go to church before deciding whether we ourselves will attend. Guests will secretly honor us for our faithfulness. It should not be necessary for us to consult the newspaper to find what the minister's sermon subject is before deciding whether or not to attend worship. The purpose of church attendance is to thank God and to receive the gift of power which he willingly gives to those who seek him.

Personal power is available through worship, but we have to participate in order to receive it. We are wise when we make churchgoing a regular habit. In time the discipline will become one of the most rewarding experiences which each week brings.

PRAYER

We praise thee, O God, for the privilege of worship. Save us from the temptation to forget our duty to thee. Spare us from the laziness which would keep us away from church. Give us new power each hour we truly worship. In Jesus' name. *Amen.*

Read Ps. 122

4th Day

WORSHIP AS PRAISE

> *Enter into his gates with thanksgiving, and into his courts with praise.*
>
> —Ps. 100:4

There are many reasons why we attend church. Our first purpose is to praise God because he is God. We feel a sincere desire to offer thanksgiving to him for his many gifts. By hymn and prayer we make known our gratitude for all his mercies. Sometimes we go to church to find release from the burden of guilt which our sin has placed upon us;

sometimes we go to seek guidance to help us when we face critical decisions; sometimes we go to learn eternal truth from the pages of the Bible and from the lips of the preacher. These are worthy purposes, and no one need feel ashamed if any of these longings fill his mind as he makes his way to church. But the first purpose of worship is to praise God and to thank him for his goodness.

Life has meaning because God is the creator and sustainer of our world. All our attitudes are changed by the assurance that we are not alone in the struggle of life. Because God is a real being we want to praise him and we search for ways to express our gratitude.

The first chapter of Paul's letter to the Romans is an indictment of the pagan world. He sums up the sins which prevail about him: wickedness, covetousness, malice, greed, envy, murder, strife, deceit, gossip, slander, sensuality, hatred, insolence, disobedience, faithlessness, ruthlessness, and—at the end—failure to praise God and to be grateful to him for his goodness.

Paul praised God throughout his writings. He seemed often to struggle for words to sufficiently express his thankfulness. Look at some of the blessings which summon each of us to gratitude:

There is life. God has given us the privilege of living. Too often we center our thoughts upon what we do not have, forgetting that however little we possess of things or money is far more than millions of people will ever own. We may want many things, but there is little we really need. And best of all we have life. Praise God for life!

Praise God for the world. Think upon the miracle of

God's universe. The hills and the lakes cry aloud of his mercies. The seedtime and harvest give evidence of his provision for every physical need. The stars in the sky and the sunrise which heralds a new day are fashioned by his hands. Common appreciation for something wonderful and mysterious should call forth our praise.

Praise God for today. Next month and next year will take care of themselves. Give thanks that you can live and love and serve today. Thank God for what you can do, and do not worry about what you are unable to do. Accept this day as a sacred trust, and praise God because he has put the hours and minutes in your care.

We understand the conclusion which was drawn by the writer of Hebrews. Having recognized the breadth of God's mercies, he said: "Therefore let us offer the sacrifice of praise to God."

PRAYER

We praise thee, O Lord. We rejoice in the evidences of thy goodness and mercy. Accept our sacrifice of praise and thanksgiving. Help us to be worthy of all thy gifts. In Jesus' name. *Amen.*

Read Ps. 8

UNDERSTANDING THROUGH WORSHIP

> *O the depth of the riches both of the wisdom
> and knowledge of God!*
>
> —ROM. 11:33

Worship helps us to recognize the supreme power and wisdom of the Almighty. In such an attitude there is a human paradox. God gave man a mind, and it is man's duty to use that mind to interpret the mysteries of the universe. But it is also true that man's outreach is limited. When we come to the mind's horizon all that is left for us is to accept and to adore.

Whenever we attend church we are confronted by evidences of God's wisdom and knowledge. We need frequent reminders that human victories and mistakes are not the only factors in the ordering of life. We are constantly subject to discouragement when we are surrounded by the results of human selfishness and greed. We are tempted to feel a sense of hopelessness about ourselves and our world. It is then that worship makes its contribution to our daily lives. We are made aware of a wisdom which is greater than that of man; we are encouraged by a divine understanding of life's problems.

A traveler in China told of finding shelter one night in a village temple because no hotel or lodging was available. She awoke in the darkness to see moonlight streaming through the window. The rays fell on the figures of the stone gods. On every face there was a snarl and a sneer; hatred was written into every look.

Our heavenly Father sometimes seems unjust when we center our attention upon the pain and suffering which so often prevails in our world. In hours of worship we come to understand that the love of God is no less real than his might.

The sickness and suffering, the hunger and pain which are the lot of many people sometimes tempt us to conclude that God is indifferent to the events that occur on the earth. New knowledge concerning the vastness of space might lead us to believe that God is too busy with the planets and stars to be concerned about men. But in an hour of worship we are made aware of the endless providence of God. We gain an understanding and knowledge that is translated into faith. From such experiences we go out to face the world with new and satisfying personal power.

PRAYER

Teach us, O God, how to worship. Help us to understand the mysteries of thy grace. In our worship may we find guidance for the day's journey, and strength sufficient for every task. In Jesus' name. *Amen.*

Read John 14:6-12

WITNESS THROUGH WORSHIP

Without faith it is impossible to please [God].
—Heb. 11:6

When we go to church we join others in thanking God for his goodness and in expressing gratitude because he is interested in us. Our presence in the house of God gives witness to our faith in him.

It is the breath-taking conclusion of the Scriptures that God himself needs our witness of faith through worship. In his encounter with the woman of Samaria, Jesus declared that "the hour cometh, and now is, when the true worshippers shall worship the Father in spirit and in truth." Then he added, "For the Father seeketh such to worship him."

God needs surrendered men and women if his purposes for the world are to be realized. He consciously placed a limit upon his power by giving to mankind the right to decide whether or not the basic laws of the universe were to be observed.

That is why God seeks the "true worshippers" to worship him. He needs the witness of our faith as we bow in homage and praise. Whenever we enter a sanctuary or meeting house we give evidence of our confidence and trust in the One who is the source of all life.

In a church sanctuary we also give witness to the world around us that we have faith in God. Within us we may have doubts, burdens, and fears; but to the world outside our attendance is evidence that we recognize the works of the Creator and that we take our stand with those who profess faith in him.

This kind of witness is essential in our day. A large number of people in every community do not attend church. They may have asked questions again and again about the meaning of life. They may have a blurred conviction that the world requires a creator to explain it. In some moments they ask themselves whether God is not close by them as they struggle with the problems of daily living.

As we join in worship we gain strength from being part of a Christian congregation. Together we cast our vote for those things which make for a better community and a better world.

When we attend church we witness to our faith. We tell the world that we are numbered among those who believe in God. That witness is desperately needed. It is persuasive in its influence upon others.

PRAYER

Strengthen the witness which we make to others through worship, O God. Help us to seek thee in spirit and in truth. Use our devotion as a means to persuade others to confess faith in thee. In Jesus' name. *Amen.*

Read Heb. 11:1-6

THE BREADTH OF WORSHIP

> *That ye present your bodies a living sacrifice,*
> *holy, acceptable unto God, which is your*
> *reasonable service.*

> —ROM. 12:1

We believe that our bodies belong to God just as much
as do our souls, that we can serve God as well with our
bodies as we can with our minds. The human body is the
temple of the Holy Spirit, the place where the Spirit
dwells, the instrument through which the Holy Spirit does
its work.

True worship is an offering to God of our bodies and
all that we do with them. Real worship involves more
than elaborate prayers, liturgy, and ritual—it is the surrender of all we have and all we are to the One who is the
giver of life. Such worship has its focus and high moments
in church services, but it does not end there. It sees the
whole world as the temple of the living God, and every
common task as an act of adoration.

Dwight L. Moody pictured this broader concept of worship in one of his sermons:

I would not say a word to detract from the holiness of the
house of God. But let us bear in mind that every place ought
to be holy to a child of God. We ought to be as true to him
in our place of business as we are in the church. When Jacob
said, "This is the house of God, and this is the gate of
Heaven," he was under the canopy of high heaven. Any place
where God is is holy, and this putting on of another air and a

sanctimonious look when we come into the house of God is all wrong. Every place ought to be holy to a true child of God.

Whatever we do becomes an acknowledgment of the power of God when we do it in a spirit of dedication. A television critic wrote about a concert in Moscow by the New York Philharmonic Orchestra: "I could not decide whether the conducting of Leonard Bernstein was an act of worship or a salute to his country. Perhaps it was both." Mr. Bernstein gave those who watched him the impression that all he possessed was being used to make the music come alive.

The discipline of worship demands our attendance at church services. But it demands much more than that. We are privileged to acknowledge God's greatness and power by everything we do, wherever we are. We are summoned to present our bodies as "a living sacrifice." When such an attitude prevails, the work of our hands, the use of our leisure hours, the service we render, and all the common deeds of every day become an evidence of true worship.

The rewards of such worship are beyond measure. God is able to utilize a dedicated human being as a channel for his power.

PRAYER

We thank thee, O God, for all thy mercies. May the concern which is reflected in our eyes, the touch of our hands, the direction of our feet, as well as our lips, speak of our gratitude to thee. May our desire to worship thee this day bring forth our best. In Jesus' name. *Amen.*

Read Rom. 12:1-8

THE DISCIPLINE
OF FAMILY RELIGION

1st Day

CHRISTIAN MARRIAGE

Marriage is honourable.

—HEB. 13:4

The writer of Hebrews reminded the early followers of Jesus that "marriage is honourable." Christians not only were wedded to each other, but they offered the world an example of men and women who, through faith, lifted marriage and the home to new and nobler heights. In a century in which marriage was no barrier to immoral living, the followers of Jesus gave the world an example of what life ought to be. Galen, a Greek philosopher, wrote of the Christians:

They number individuals who in ruling and controlling themselves, in their keen pursuit of virtue, and in their faithfulness to the family, have attained a pitch not inferior to that of real philosophers.

The marks of a Christian marriage have not changed. Scientific advances have transformed the furnishings within a house, but they have not altered the rules which make a dwelling into a home.

Faithfulness to marriage vows is a mark of Christian devotion. Changing attitudes toward sex in our day point to the need for integrity in Christian marriage. There are no exceptions to the rules which demand purity and honor. The laws of the state are designed to protect the home, but more is involved than civil law. A union made by the church requires faithfulness on the part of each one who takes the vows.

Religion is important to a happy home. While husband and wife may not belong to the same church (though experience indicates that successful marriages occur more often when the family attends church together), vital religion will be a daily experience in the home. Every couple can have a church in their house. Religious customs differ with each family. Usually they include grace before meals and some form of family devotions. When these practices are accompanied by a love for one another and a kindly concern for the welfare of all, a Christian home is assured.

"Marriage is honourable." Christian marriage gives the expectation of happiness to husband and wife, to parents and children. Best of all, it brings the presence of God to bless the home with spiritual power.

PRAYER

We are grateful, O Lord, for the joys of marriage and family life. We thank thee for our homes and for the example of those who love us. Help us to be faithful to the vows which will make our home a place of happiness. Give spiritual power to guide us in the way we should go. In Jesus' name. *Amen.*

Read *Prov. 4:1-13*

2nd Day

A HERITAGE OF FAITH

Call to remembrance the former days.

—HEB. 10:32

The early followers of Jesus experienced many difficult hours. They were persecuted for their faith; their families were ridiculed, their homes ransacked, and their possessions destroyed. They walked the streets of their cities with jeers ringing in their ears. They met these trials with bravery and perseverance, and they remained loyal to Christ.

When life was easier many drifted away from the faith; the pleasures of the world became attractive. No longer were Christians marked as different from people around them. The writer of Hebrews asked them to "call to remembrance the former days."

Most of the early Christians came from a Jewish background. Their heritage made the sanctity of family life a precious part of their past. Their faith was a shared experience with those they loved. We, too, are wise if we "call to remembrance the former days." Many of us can trace the beginnings of our faith to a home where God was real. The moment of conversion or personal experience of the presence of Christ may have occurred in a church, but the foundations were usually laid at home.

It is not strange that many Christians point to the religion of their mothers as the most influential fact in their lives. A department store in Philadelphia recently provided a window display which attracted wide attention. There were large portraits of the mothers of ten famous Americans, among them, Theodore Roosevelt, Calvin Coolidge, Dwight L. Moody, Abraham Lincoln, and William McKinley. Each mother's picture was in a large frame, and in one corner was inserted a miniature photograph of her famous son. In the center of the display a basket of food and an open Bible symbolized the two vital contributions of mothers to the lives of these men who grew to greatness.

Sometimes it is a father whose faith and honesty gives meaning to faith. John Wanamaker, the department store executive, often told of the evening prayers which were conducted in the farm home in Scotland where he was born. His father read the Bible to the assembled family, then led them in fervent prayer as the family knelt together on the floor of the living room. Wanamaker declared: "I lived carelessly at times, but I never could get too far away from the influence of my godly father."

Children need an encounter with the presence of God in their homes. In future years they should be able to "call to remembrance the former days" and possess memories which mark the beginnings of a faith sufficient to guide them in the years ahead.

PRAYER

We are grateful, O God, when we call to remembrance the former days. Our heritage is one of faith. We are grateful for the religion which was made real in our homes. Help us to encourage devotion to thy will in those who live within our family circle. In Jesus' name. *Amen.*

Read Ps. 107:1-15

3rd Day

REVERENCE BEGINS IN THE HOME

> *Let them learn first to shew piety at home.*
> —I TIM. 5:4

We live in an age marked by a sharp increase of delinquency and crime among youth. Anxious public officials often point to the church and the school as the agencies in the community that hold the answer to the problem. It is important that the church and the school meet their obligations to growing youth, for these are essential to the development of character. But their efforts must be supplemented by what happens in the home.

When religion is made a vital part of family life, both parents and children will feel reverence as they are aware

32

of God's presence and goodness. A lack of reverence is at the root of all individual and social evil.

It is natural for children to feel a sense of awe before the mysterious world around them; it is unnatural for children to be rebellious and hostile. Most psychologists who study personality include the instinct for religion among the basic drives which control human development. While all children respond naturally to the idea of God as the divine power at the center of all life, there is a conflict within them between the tendency to submit to the will of God and the desire to gain selfish ends. They fight against anything which threatens to deprive them of what they want. When they learn reverence for God early in life, they tend to submerge their selfish desires.

How can reverence become a controlling factor in family life?

First, the thought of God must be constantly kept before the family. If religious faith has no place in daily conversations in the home, it is reasonable to expect that the members of the family will have no vital religious awareness. If the family talk is centered on money, gadgets, and the importance of social position, it is inevitable that growing children will assume that these are the most important values in life.

The practice of saying grace before meals is the most widely used method to remind family groups that God is real. When this discipline becomes a set habit in a home then at least three times every day both parents and children are reminded that God is the source of all they possess.

Many families make a circle of hands around the table

as the prayer is offered. This custom reminds each member of the family of their unity in the faith which is expressed.

Practices vary as to the way the grace is given. Often the children say the prayer in turn. The experience may be valuable as a way to teach growing youth the habit of vocal prayer. There is much to be said for the custom of having the father say the grace. His voice at such a time is a witness to the fact that the head of the house puts his confidence in the providence of God. Perhaps it is wise to vary the procedure to avoid the formalism which may become meaningless.

Family religion, or the absence of it, is the key to many serious problems which confront the modern home. The admonition which Paul gave in the first century is just as valid today: "Let them first learn to shew piety at home."

PRAYER

We give thanks, O God, that thy presence may be known no less in a house than in a church. Help us to be truly reverent before thy mercies. Make our lives a witness which will speak of faith to those we love. In Jesus' name. *Amen.*

Read I Tim. 5:1-4

THE NOBLEST PRIVILEGE OF FAMILY LIFE

*In whom we have boldness and access with
confidence by the faith of him.*

—EPH. 3:12

A group of scientists were concerned with defining the
difference between the lower animals and man. Anthro-
pologists, zoologists, and psychologists disagreed in their
conclusions. Each found in the animals certain character-
istics that make them like mankind. It remained for a
commission of experts to decide that man is the only
creature who seeks something beyond himself and his
world. He is not bound by the earth; he yearns for fellowship with God.

It is our nature that we live in a world of space and time;
and we live in a world of mind and spirit. We are spirit-
ually poor when our personal and family interests and
affections become so absorbed in the world of things that
we forget the world of the spirit.

The discipline of daily devotions has proved one of the
best means by which both adults and growing youth can
keep enduring values in proper perspective. A religion
which is reserved for Sunday is not sufficient to hold back
the pressures of the world. The human spirit needs a day-
by-day reminder of the presence and power of God. When
this experience comes in a family group, it has added meaning.

No family undertakes daily devotions without encoun-
tering certain problems. When children are young, parents

can easily arrange to have devotions at the close of a meal or at bedtime. But as boys and girls grow older, and activities multiply, the problem of a suitable time becomes more serious.

If there is one meal in the day when parents and children are together it is perhaps the best opportunity for Bible reading and prayer. Some families get up fifteen minutes earlier in the morning to share devotions.

It has been traditional for the father to lead in family prayers. This custom has much to commend it. In many families, however, each member leads the devotions in turn. Sometimes they are a shared responsibility with one person reading the Bible, another reading from a devotional book, and each one leading in a brief prayer. Widespread participation helps to keep the attention of all who share in the experience.

The question is often raised as to what should be the content of family devotions. In general, a reading from the Bible and prayer are the two elements which always need to be included.

Many families read from a devotional book which gives sight into the Bible passage or which provides illustrans to relate the passage to daily living. *The Upper Room* idely used for this purpose. Sometimes a book which ws a specific theme will answer the needs of a par r family.

writer of Ephesians tells us that we have "boldness ess with confidence" to the presence of God. At first rds seem an indication of arrogance. But the in-

36

vitation is established on firm grounds. Jesus opened the way through which any family, by praying in his name and by fellowship with him, is lifted out of the world of selfish striving to catch a glimpse of the world of the spirit.

Daily devotions are the method, and Jesus Christ is the way, by which we claim the noblest privileges of family life.

PRAYER

Help us, O Lord, to take time this day to seek thee. In the seeking, help our family to dwell for a time in the world of the spirit. Through Jesus Christ our Lord, we pray. *Amen.*

Read Ps. 119:57-64

5th Day

WHEN A FAMILY IS DEDICATED TO GOD

By faith Abraham. . . .

—HEB. 11:17

When John Bunyan was in jail he thought a great deal about what would happen to his family if he were to be hanged. He was especially concerned for the future of his little blind daughter. He wrote: "I saw in this condition I was a man who was pulling down his house upon the head of his wife and children; yet, I thought, I must do it, I must do it. I must trust God, and leave those I love in His hands."

Much of the tension which disturbs family life will be avoided if we turn our homes and families over to the guidance of God. Selfishness is the source of many of the troubles which beset the modern home. Sons and daughters demand the pleasures of the world without inquiring whether the practices involved are in keeping with the standards of the family. Money, clothes, and popularity become more important than the welfare of the home.

The attitude of parents usually determines the trend which the lives of their children will take—but not always. Parents have generally less opportunity to shape the character of their children in this generation, as more time and interests—even for small children—are devoted to neighborhood and community activities. Boys and girls have more freedom today. They are influenced by the forces which play upon them outside the home.

It still remains true, however, that the dedication of parents to the will of God makes a lasting impact on the children. They are quick to sense insincerity. When a boy in a pastor's training class was asked why he failed to cooperate with the group, he burst out to say: "This religious stuff is bunk." The pastor traced the source of the reaction to the father of the boy who, while a member and regular attendant at church, shouted in anger at his wife, and often turned at such moments upon the boy to strike him for imaginary disobedience. It was useles to talk to the boy of a just and loving God. He knew the heavenly Father was not like that because his own father believed in God, and he was neither just nor loving.

When a home and family are dedicated, the divine spirit

will be seen not only in shared experiences of family devotions and church attendance, but in the daily attitudes of husband and wife toward each other and toward the children. The house and the family, the present and the future will all be regarded as a sacred trust because God has been the giver.

The Christian faith challenges us to consecrate our homes and families to God. Abraham left an example of one who was willing to trust the child he loved to the God whom he served. He discovered that the threat of disaster was merely a step toward greater joy and faith. Life was enriched when they walked together as a family in complete surrender to the will of the heavenly Father.

PRAYER

Help us, O Lord, to put our trust in thee. May our homes be brightened by a family which is dedicated to the doing of thy will. May we love one another better because we love thee. In Jesus' name. *Amen.*

Read Gen. 17:1-8

FAITH AS THE KEY TO A PEACEFUL HOME

There remaineth therefore a rest to the people of God.

—HEB. 4:9

Family life is often strained in this generation. Behind the word "incompatability," which appears so frequently in the divorce courts, there is a world of tension and disagreement, of argument and bitterness. Too often we attribute the tensions to differences in personality. Such differences do exist, and they require understanding and patience; but we must look farther to explain much of the trouble which stalks the modern home. Frequently it arises from a failure to share common interests. Each member of the family is traveling a different road, absorbed in his own problems. Having no ground of common interest it is inevitable that he should be impatient with those who seem unconcerned by what he does.

Happy family life requires a unity of purpose and concern in whatever is undertaken by each one separately. Children have a right to the interest of their parents in their activities. They are individuals. They grow with each new experience; their horizons expand by every new undertaking. When they feel alone in the struggle they tend to become aloof or bitter. They look for satisfactions outside the home.

It may seem strange that the answer to these problems is found best in a vital faith in God and in a sense of dedication to his purposes. When a father has faith, his work becomes a sacred trust which is of concern to members of his family because they, too, recognize the holiness of their father's occupation. When a mother has faith in God her household responsibilities become an expression of her loyalty. When children believe in God their school work and their recreation are carried on as a part of their religious life. Unworthy activities are ruled out. What they try to accomplish deserves the interest of each member of the family.

A continuing sense of Christian dedication will make for peace. All the family has and all the family does will be in keeping with the will of God. Selfishness will gradually disappear. Because each one is endeavoring to do what God would have him do tensions will be at a minimum. Sharp words will be silenced even before they are uttered.

The Christian home is a place of rest. It becomes a haven to which each member of the family comes, certain that he will find understanding and peace. This is the only kind of rest which will overcome the noisy and demanding pressures of life in our day.

PRAYER

O God, we thank thee for the rest which we find in our homes. Help us to be faithful to thee, and through our faith to help those who love us to find rest from their daily struggles. Guide us into the ways by which we may do thy will in our homes. In Jesus' name. *Amen.*

Read Heb. 4:4-9

41

FAMILY RELIGION ON SUNDAY

> *He that regardeth the day, regardeth it unto the Lord.*
>
> —Rom. 14:6

Mary Slessor spent three lonely years as a missionary in Africa. She saw no person except the natives who lived in the jungle village that was her place of service. Because she had no calendar she sometimes confused the days. Once she found she had held religious services on Monday. At another time she hammered away on the roof of her house on Sunday, not realizing it was the Sabbath.

Few of us would question whether the services were any the less helpful because they were held on Monday, or that Mary Slessor was in any sense breaking the commandments because she was working on Sunday. Yet the Lord's Day is sacred. Something of vital significance is lost when Sunday is no different from any other day in the week.

Many Christian families are puzzled to know what is right and proper for the followers of Jesus to do on this day. The problem becomes more serious with each passing decade.

Sunday is both the Lord's day and the day when the family is privileged to spend time together. The pressures of our world tend to divide the family. Parents and children are busy. It is not uncommon to hear of families which are never together at any time during the week. Father has his work and his committee meetings; mother has her community and church obligations; the children have their clubs, rehearsals, and parties. The discipline of family life demands that one day be set aside as the time when parents and children will share common interests and joys.

A Christian family will devote a large part of Sunday to the worship, study, and fellowship opportunities at the church. Everyone should attend church school and the regular services of worship. If the entire family group is engaged in these activities at the same time the danger of revolt is lessened.

Some families walk in a park or along a country road on Sunday afternoon. A ride to explore a spot of historical or natural interest is often rewarding. When children are young the day becomes a rare opportunity to read aloud some of the great books of the ages. Wise planning will uncover numerous activities which will be of interest. The important consideration is to find ways to give individual happiness as well as an opportunity to enjoy shared experiences.

As Christians we do not worship a day, we worship the God who gave us the day. Our loving Father, with infinite care, created time for our use. We wisely set aside, as did our fathers, a period for rest and worship. But God created Monday, and Tuesday, and all the rest of the week. A Christian family finds the true values of Christian living when it accepts every day as a holy trust and uses each one for worship and service.

PRAYER

Guide us, O God, into the paths of wisdom and knowledge. Teach us how wisely to use the Sabbath day. May our example be a witness to the faith which is within us. Pour thy power upon us that we may be strong to do thy will. In Jesus' name. *Amen.*

Read Ps. 85:6-13

THE DISCIPLINE
OF BIBLE READING

1st Day

A SECRET OF SPIRITUAL GROWTH

> *That we henceforth be no more children,*
> *tossed to and fro. . . . But speaking the truth in*
> *love, may grow up into him in all things,*
> *which is the head, even Christ.*

> —EPH. 4:14, 15

Many Christians never grow up. They remain beginners in the faith. The time and the effort required to secure the treasures of the spiritual life call for too much effort; the moral and social demands of loyalty to Christ cost more than they are prepared to pay; so they remain children in the faith.

Christians are committed to grow in knowledge. There are those who declare that a faith which was good enough for their fathers is good enough for them. Some followers of Jesus boast of beliefs which have not developed in twenty, thirty, or forty years. There are mature men and women who are content with the religious understanding of a child. The mysteries of God await the eager seeker; the treasures of Christ are available to one who learns of him;

the truth of the Bible is open to those who spend time each day reading its matchless pages.

We are wise if we make the Bible our daily companion. Some Christians carry a small New Testament in their pockets or purses. Many men keep a Bible on the desk in their office or on their work bench. Numerous homes have a Bible at all times on the kitchen table or in the living room. The value of each of these practices lies in the fact that the Bible is immediately available to be read. A few moments snatched during a lull in activity become an opportunity to read a short passage.

Often a few verses read slowly are of greater value than a chapter which is hurried through. One of the amazing qualities of the Bible is that a single verse may possess the secret of more spiritual power than an entire secular book devoted to ways of gaining happiness. We are wise if we read slowly, uttering a silent prayer that God may speak to us through his Word.

The new translations are helpful for devotional reading. They enable us to share the thinking of a scholar who has spent many years grappling with an ancient language with which most of us are unfamiliar.

Our reading of the Bible should make us want to memorize certain verses and chapters. Most of the passages which we can repeat from memory were learned before we were twelve years old. Memorization is more difficult after we enter our teens. Yet ability to learn is not so much involved as is concentration. A treasure of personal power is at hand when great verses from the Bible are firmly fixed in our minds to be immediately available for any moment of need.

We grow in knowledge and faith when we make the Bible our daily companion. Divine truth becomes an unfailing source of personal power. The mysteries of life and suffering and eternity are cleared.

PRAYER

Thou hast made us to grow, O Lord. Thy grace has given us the spiritual food we need. Help us to follow the spiritual discipline which sends us to the Bible again and again for the strength which comes from its pages. May we walk in the light of thy truth. In Jesus' name. *Amen.*

Read Prov. 4:1-18

2nd Day

A REVELATION IN WORDS

> *Whatsoever things were written aforetime were written for our learning.*
>
> —ROM. 15:4

Loyalty to the Christian faith has always demanded the study of scripture. Reading the Bible has been a spiritual discipline for faithful followers of Jesus in every generation.

The apostle Paul reminds us that the Bible tells of God's

47

dealings with people. It is a record which demonstrates that it is always better to be right with God and to suffer than to be wrong with men and to avoid trouble. The history of Israel is used to demonstrate the assurance that good eventually triumphs and evil is defeated. The Bible declares to us that God's way is not always the easy way, but that it is the only enduring way to discover those values which make life worthwhile for time and for eternity.

Nations live or die by the manner in which they respond to the laws which are written into the Bible. A historian attempted to explain Spain's waning power in the New World in the seventeenth century by the growing influence of Britain. He concluded that Spain had gone to North America seeking for treasures of gold, while English colonists were seeking for opportunities to worship God. When Spain became the shadow of what was once a great nation, someone must have opened the Bible to read: "Every one that heareth these sayings of mine, and doeth them not, shall be likened unto a foolish man, which built his house upon the sand."

The Bible shows individuals and nations how to live. Sometimes the words seem unpleasant. They make us uncomfortable; they rebuke our selfishness. But they are true to life. To neglect their challenge brings death; to accept their truth assures us of life.

The Bible holds before us the promises of God. It is said that Ian Maclaren chose a verse each day when he began a round of pastoral calls. He would leave the passage in each home, urging the members of the family to take it with them wherever they went.

The promises of God cover every moment of personal need: they give courage in weakness, comfort in sorrow, faith in moments of doubt. Who can fail to be strengthened in hours of disaster when he is assured that "the eternal God is thy refuge, and underneath are the everlasting arms"? Who can feel there is no hope for sinful men when he remembers that Christ is able "to save them to the uttermost that come unto God by him"? Who can think that death is final when he hears again the words: "O Death, where is thy sting? O grave, where is thy victory? Thanks be to God, which giveth us the victory through our Lord Jesus Christ"? Who can neglect the opportunities to read the Bible and to pray when he is reminded that "he that dwelleth in the secret place of the most High shall abide under the shadow of the almighty"?

The promises of the Word of God are life and strength for all who take the opportunity to learn and to test their truth. They give assurance of spiritual power to meet every need.

PRAYER

We thank thee, O God, for thy truth. Help us today to listen to thy message as written in the pages of the Bible. Feed us with the spiritual food which gives us life. In Jesus' name. *Amen.*

Read Matt. 7:21-28

THE DEEPER EXPERIENCES OF
BIBLE READING

When for the time ye ought to be teachers, ye have need that one teach you again.

—Heb. 5:12

The Bible is a source of knowledge for anyone who is eager to understand the Christian faith. Within its pages we discover a key to the nature of God, as well as the secret of how to live. Too often we asume that all we have to do is to read the Bible at random to gain the ends we seek.

The full treasure of personal power in the Bible is reserved for those who go beyond a casual reading of the book. When one is familiar with the message of the various chapters, he can turn immediately to the portion which has significance for a particular occasion or need. No Christian should stand among the hills or mountains without wanting to read again the 121st psalm. Every moment of doubt should make the sixth chapter of Matthew a new challenge to faith. Creeping malice or hatred should send a follower of Jesus back to the thirteenth chapter of I Corinthians. The awareness of a heavy load of responsibility should make the fortieth chapter of Isaiah an eagerly sought out source of encouragement. Familiarity with the Bible increases its ability to give the help which the moment calls for.

There is no short cut to this kind of experience. Lists of passages which deal with specific problems are helpful, but they are a poor substitute for the knowledge which is gathered by the regular discipline of Bible reading.

Every book in the Bible came out of a particular need. Each of the Gospels tells the story of the revelation of God in Christ, but each one had a different purpose and was directed to a different audience. The letters of Paul were shaped by the special problems which existed in the cities to which they were addressed. It is an evidence of divine inspiration in scripture that so many passages prove helpful to the reader, even if he is ignorant concerning the purpose of the author and the needs of people which gave rise to the book. However, it should be clear that the rewards of Bible reading are multiplied when we are acquainted with the origin of each book.

Intelligent Bible reading requires the use of helps. A commentary and a Bible dictionary are practical tools. No generation has possessed a finer aid to understanding than we have in *The Interpreter's Bible.* We grow when we appropriate the wisdom gained by the scholars.

Growing children receive insight into the sometimes difficult passages by the use of Bible storybooks. Commentaries and storybooks are never a substitute for the Bible itself, but they provide the added information which enables us to unearth its treasures.

We add to our insights when we have a teacher. It is a privilege for a Christian to be a member of a class in the church school or a Bible study group. One lifetime is too short to learn all that is revealed in the Word of God. We are wise when we use every available opportunity to add to our store of knowledge.

PRAYER

Dear Father, forgive us for our carelessness toward thy truth. Help us to be more faithful students of thy Word. Make us restless until our faith is anchored to the rock of certainty. We seek thy will for our lives. Help us to follow it. In Jesus' name. *Amen.*

Read I Cor. 15:27-34

4th Day

THE LIVING WORD

For the word of God is quick.

—HEB. 4:12

The word "quick" was used by the author of Hebrews to describe the Bible. The word has only a remote relationship to what we mean when we say something is "quick." Yet the word is not unfamiliar to us. Millions of Christians use it every time they repeat the Apostles' Creed: "From thence he shall come to judge the quick and the dead."

One scholar translates the word "quick" as "living"; another phrases it as "instinct with life." They remind us that the Bible breathes life from each of its pages. Many books, although they may have had meaning for the generation in which they were written, are now dead. That is not true of the Bible. It pulsates with a message which is significant for our day.

The Bible is a sacred book. That is why it has so often been enclosed in a cover of black leather with gilt edges— it seems an appropriate binding for the message of God to mankind. Yet the somber covering increases our temptation to think that it belongs to a cherished but dead past. It multiplies the danger of passing by the Bible to take up a magazine or a novel.

The writer of Hebrews tells us that the Bible has a living message for men in every age. Political issues which are current may seem momentous, but they will soon be forgotten. The work of a few novelists may live long enough to become the object of study by scholars, but the Word of God is of continued interest in every generation. It will speak to the hearts of men when books which absorb the attention of people in the twentieth century have been forgotten.

Human nature does not change from age to age. The difference between right and wrong is as clear today as in the year 1000 B.C. The man who wears a space suit when he climbs into a rocket for a plunge into outer space has the same moral problems which Abraham faced when he climbed on the back of a camel to start a journey into a land which was strange and forbidding. Faith and integrity are as necessary now as they were then.

The guilt which David felt when he allowed lust to make him forget what was right and honorable is the same guilt which pursues an unfaithful man in the twentieth century. The same forgiveness which was offered to Mary Magdalene is offered to penitent sinners in our day.

Worry and fear are widespread in this generation. Material abundance is never a protection against their pressing power. But people were worried and afraid in the first century, and the resources which Jesus offered them through trust in the goodness of God are even now the most effective antidote for the worries and fears which haunt us.

The Bible is alive. We receive strength when we steep our minds in the message which flows from its pages.

PRAYER

We thank thee, O God, for thy truth as revealed in the Bible. Thy life is in its pages. Help us to find thee as we read and meditate upon thy Word. In Jesus' name. *Amen.*

Read Acts 7:44-50

5th Day

THE PENETRATING POWER OF SCRIPTURE

For the word of God is . . . powerful.
—HEB. 4:12

In the original Greek text the word "powerful" did not mean explosive, but, rather, penetrating. The writer is saying that the Bible is not so much like a hydrogen bomb as like an X ray which penetrates deep into the human body to heal a cancer.

Some passages emphasize the power within the Bible to

demolish our false ideas of what life ought to be. Here the message is different. The power of the Bible is its ability to get under our cloak of respectability to find what is in our hearts.

The Bible penetrates our spiritual life to discover whether it is genuine. It makes us inquire of ourselves whether we merely go through the motions of worship. It forces us to look closely at our moral life and stirs feelings of revulsion when our deeds are unworthy of the faith we profess.

Some have likened the Word of God to a searchlight, for it picks out those who are engaged in evil practices. It focuses on the nation which is interested in furthering selfish ends.

The writer of Hebrews, however, saw the Bible as more than a searchlight. A searchlight illuminates only what can be seen, while the Bible reveals the heart of a person or a nation. It lets us see ourselves as we really are; and if we are made ashamed of what we find, its mission is partially fulfilled. Then it shows us what life ought to be.

The mission of the Bible is to deal, not only with deeds, but with motives. Jesus frequently seemed to treat lightly what appeared to be the obvious evil, then went on to examine the inner purposes which were involved. When Mary Magdalene was dragged before him, the weight of condemnation rested no heavier upon her than upon her accusers. Jesus made them see their lives as they really were.

Paul wrote bluntly about the evil practices which he observed in many of the communities which he visited, but when he wrote to the Galatians he was persuasive and tender. He did not rail against them for specific sins, but he led the followers of Jesus to examine their inner hearts for evidences of unfaithfulness.

The enduring quality of the Bible is explained in part by its ability to make all of us look closely at our real selves. If it had dealt merely with evils which were current at the time the books were written it would long since have been forgotten. But scripture does more than that. It not only declares that a course of action is wrong; it makes us examine the lack of surrender which permits us to do evil.

The Bible is a practical guide for daily living. Sometimes it strikes with the sharpness of a two-edged sword, ripping away our cloak of false virtue. Yet it never leaves us wounded by our sins. It offers cleansing and forgiveness and a new kind of life.

The Word of God is "powerful." We are wise if we come regularly under the focus of its penetrating and healing rays.

PRAYER

Dear Father, we need thy Word. We wander into pathways which are out of keeping with thy will. Give us a listening ear to catch the warnings in the Bible. Help us to model our lives after the pattern which thy Word has given us. In Jesus' name. *Amen.*

Read Phil. 2:12-16

THE ANCHOR WHICH HOLDS

> *Therefore we ought to give the more earnest*
> *heed to the things which we have heard, lest*
> *at any time we should let them slip.*
>
> —HEB. 2:1

The greatest threat to our faith is not that we become atheists overnight, but that we carelessly drift into attitudes in which God is forgotten. Few people deliberately deny their faith; they wander slowly away from God. Not many Christians choose a single moment to renounce the Bible; they stray farther from the influence of its teachings by failing to read it. There are not many people who commit a serious crime which ruins their lives; there are thousands who, day by day, become involved in unworthy practices which finally lead to doubt and guilt.

Jay Deiss likened a board room in a large corporation to the vestry of an imposing church. The room had character. It suggested honesty and dependability. But the atmosphere gave no protection against the scheming for power, the jealousy, and the plotting for position which occurred whenever the board met. So we often try to conceal our worldliness in an atmosphere which we hope will seem religious. It is tempting to justify dishonest practices by arguing that our deeds will benefit others. A man who was arrested for embezzlement pleaded that he had used the money to help people who were in need. A football coach whose university was charged with dishonesty in recruiting players lamely pleaded that he was doing it for the welfare of his alma mater. These practices do not differ from those of the slave trader in the last century who attended church upon his return from an expedition and thanked God that he was able to rescue the poor men and women from the jungles of Africa.

We need, not an atmosphere of piety, but God-directed lives. Our generation calls for men who will not talk about honesty, but who will be honest. The spread of Christianity awaits those who will not only speak loudly of a need for religion, but who will share the truth of Christ wherever they go.

The Bible continues to be our best guide. It belongs in our homes; it pleads to be taken into business. Its teachings must be observed in every social gathering. An atmosphere of holiness is not enough—we need the Bible and its message as a guide and strength for daily living.

All of us are wise when we anchor our lives to the rock of faith, keeping our thoughts and acts squared by the truth which is revealed in the Bible. God will then become a living presence, and the duties which each day brings will have new meaning.

PRAYER

Dear Father, we would anchor our lives to the certainties which are revealed in thy Word. Save us from the temptation to drift into doubt and evil. In our finer moments we want to be thine and to do thy will. Accept our dedication of life to thee. In Jesus' name. *Amen.*

Read Heb. 2:1-4

THE REWARDS OF BIBLE READING

> *Nevertheless the foundation of God standeth sure.*
>
> —II TIM. 2:19

The discipline of Bible reading has many rewards, not the least of which is the discovery of the foundations of faith upon which a satisfying life can be built. We often hear of those who are seeking for a philosophy of life. They grope through the writings of ancient sages or devour the teachings of the leaders of the world's religions. There are rewards to be gained from such a search, but the experience of millions of men testifies that the Bible holds the key to a complete understanding of life at its best.

We live in a questioning age. Men want to know the secrets of the universe as well as the meaning of human existence. The worth of the Bible is not undermined by questions concerning its values, but much is lost if that is the only attitude of the seeker. The late G. K. Chesterton once said: "We have found all the questions that can be found. It is time we stopped looking for questions and started looking for answers." The time has come to seek answers to the problems which confront us.

The conversion of Augustine occurred when he opened the Bible at random and came upon a passage in Romans 13. He had been walking in a garden. Troubled because he had failed to live a good life, he cried out: "How long? How long? Tomorrow and tomorrow—why not now? Why not this hour and an end to my weakness?" As he wept he heard a voice which sounded like a child's, saying: "Take and read; take and read." Augustine hurried back to where he had left his Bible, and, as he wrote:

I snatched it up and read the first passage my eyes fell on: "Let us not walk in revelry and drunkenness, in immorality and in shamelessness, in contention and in strife. But put ye on the Lord Jesus Christ." I neither wished nor needed to read further. With the end of that sentence, as though the light of assurance had poured into my heart, all the shades of doubt were scattered.

The matchless prose and poetry of the Bible speaks to the needs of men in every age. Its stories and teachings deal with the experience of those facing every type of problem. It differs from other books—it confronts us with life as it really is. The divine element is introduced to give meaning to our struggles and to provide strength for our daily tasks.

When our ears are tuned to hear its message, the Bible answers the age-old questions about our origin and destiny.

Drawing upon the experience of men in every human situation, it points out truth about God and about the ways of life which hold the greatest hope for happiness. Best of all, the Bible gives assurance that "the foundations of God standeth sure."

Open your Bible each day with an expectant heart. Read its pages eagerly. You will find the personal guidance and power which will make life triumphant.

PRAYER

Dear Father, we thank thee for the eternal truth which
has been entrusted to us in the Bible. We will take time
this day to listen to thy voice. Speak to us through thy
Word. In Jesus' name. *Amen.*

Read II Tim. 1:1-16

THE DISCIPLINE
OF PRAYER

1st Day

PRAYER IS GOD'S GIFT

Keep that which is committed to thy trust.
—I TIM. 6:20

Major Samuel Tyson guided a crippled airliner through five hectic hours before ditching the plane with its eighty passengers in the stormy Pacific. Every life was saved. For his bravery he was awarded the Distinguished Service Cross. Someone asked him what he thought about during the hours while he waited for the moment of crash. He replied: "God, love, family, living, mistakes, achievements, faults, assets: I made many resolutions, and I did a lot of praying."

Tragedy tends to strip away all the nonessentials to permit us to see life as it really is. We recognize the futility of much that we do. We feel a compulsion to use the days and the years that are left for that which is best and enduring. We turn in such moments to prayer.

It is a human tragedy that prayer is often reserved for periods of sorrow or trial. We turn to God at such a time when few thoughts of prayer have entered our minds while life was smooth and pleasant.

The root of the problem may be that we never have escaped the Old Testament idea of God. We think of him as aloof and distant. We may even assume that he is indifferent to our joys and sorrows. When life collapses about us we forget that God seems far removed and cry out for the power which only he can give us. After the crisis has passed we slip back into the assumption that God is beyond our reach or concern.

Jesus gave us an example of a life which centered in prayer. The New Testament reminds us that he prayed in connection with every crucial event in his public ministry. He prayed on the Mount of Temptation; he prayed when he used God's power to heal; he prayed on the mountain when long hours of teaching had sapped his strength; he prayed at the Last Supper; he prayed in Gethsemane; he prayed on the cross. Anyone who accepts the example and teachings of Jesus as a key to the abundant life must become a person who prays.

The frequent return of Jesus to prayer is of even greater significance because of what it tells us about God. Our Master assures us that the heavenly Father is always approachable. Rites or ceremonies are unnecessary to command his attention: he is at hand whenever we speak his name in earnest prayer.

Moreover, Jesus made it clear that the privilege of talking to the heavenly Father is granted to everyone who is willing to bow in his presence. The humblest seeker has the same standing as the highest priest. None of us need feel that God is unconcerned with our problems; no event is outside the reach of our Father's interest.

The privilege of prayer has been given to each of us. We are wise if we learn its secrets. Personal power is the mark of the Christian who really prays.

PRAYER

Dear Father, teach us to pray. We seek thy presence to bless our daily lives. The mystery of thy love leaves us without words to express our gratitude. Help us this day to seek thy presence and to walk in the light of thy truth. In Jesus' name. *Amen.*

Read I Tim. 6:1-20

2nd Day

DAILY EXPERIENCES OF PRAYER

Continuing instant in prayer.

—Rom. 12:12

Every Christian should have certain times each day when it is his custom to pray. Many faithful followers of Jesus set aside periods in the early morning. It is a healthy religion which kindles the desire to give thanks to God in the morning for the gift of a new day, and which makes us seek divine guidance as we go to work or to school. Again, it is natural to pray when the day has come to an end. A Christian ought to be aware of the need to thank God for all that the day has brought. It is natural that we should plead for forgiveness when we are conscious of the mistakes and failures which have marked our relationships with others. The peace that follows true penitence is a far better preparation for sleep than the gnawing feelings of guilt which keep us awake long hours during the night.

Many businessmen and office workers are using daily coffee breaks as a time to pray. Some housewives pause at set times in their work to follow the discipline of prayer.

Other religions of the world sometimes make Christians humble by the devotion of their followers to habits of prayer. A recent traveler in Turkey tells of riding a bus from Istanbul to Ankara. The driver brought the vehicle to a sudden stop in wild country far removed from any village. Several of the passengers left their seats to go outside. Each one spread a small rug on the ground and knelt to say his prayers. After a few moments they returned to the bus and the journey continued.

Our proud assertions that God does not demand a fixed hour for prayer are valid, but too often a lack of discipline results in failure to pray at all.

We ought to pray often. We can whisper a word of thanks when we walk under the beauty of God's skies. Praise and thanksgiving should be as natural to us as breathing. We can whisper a plea for wisdom as we approach an interview or a class in school. We can ask for and receive God's help as we undertake a difficult task.

A businessman in Pennsylvania is subject to severe stress and strain. When faced with a situation which undermines his strength he recalls a stanza from a hymn written by John Greenleaf Whittier:

Drop thy still dews of quietness,
    Till all our strivings cease;
Take from our souls the strain and stress,
And let our ordered lives confess
    The beauty of Thy peace.

He tells us that he whispers this prayer at least once every day.

Frank Laubach suggests the use of what he calls "flash prayers." They are single phrases or sentences devoted to praise or thanksgiving, petition or intercession. They may be spoken aloud or kept within the mind.

Every thought and deed is a form of prayer when we dedicate our lives to God. He is present in the Holy Spirit whenever a follower of Jesus endeavors to do his will. Vocal prayer is essential, but a totally surrendered man or woman is "continuing instant in prayer."

PRAYER

Kindle our spirits, O God, to the awareness of thy presence. Help us to use wisely the opportunity which thou hast put within us for fellowship with thee. May our lives no less praise thee than our lips. In Jesus' name. *Amen.*

Read Rom. 12:1-12

THE SCHOOL OF PRAYER

> *I beseech you, brethren, for the Lord Jesus Christ's sake, and for the love of the Spirit, that ye strive together with me in your prayers to God for me.*
>
> —Rom. 15:30

The mysteries of prayer are not solved in a day. Every faithful Christian is enrolled in a school of prayer. We may pass from a lower grade to a higher grade as we grow in knowledge and experience, but few of us ever qualify for graduation.

The apostle Paul earned the right to speak on the subject of prayer, for he learned the secret in the crucible of experience. He suggests four important principles to guide those who would learn how to communicate with God.

First, effectiveness in prayer is a matter of intense effort. Paul tells us to "strive" in our prayers. Some of us rush into the presence of God expecting to command him to do our will. We think of prayer as getting what we want when our own abilities have proved inadequate. Whatever may be the rewards of such an approach, they do not reveal the true values of communion with God. We know that genuine prayer is a matter of striving. We must work in order to know God, to learn his will, and to receive his gift of power.

Second, we must expect to encounter times when God seems not to be listening. Few Christians escape certain moments when faith seems unreal. At such times we go through the motions of prayer, but there is no awareness of God's presence. Church services offer little help. We feel alone, bewildered, and discouraged.

During the arid moments we will be strengthened if we continue to worship and serve. There may be little joy in singing in the choir, but we keep steadfastly at it. The satisfactions of teaching a class may have been replaced by a tremendous sense of burden, but we faithfully persevere. The earlier pleasure of fellowship with friends may have been forgotten, but we force ourselves to continue sharing opportunities to be with the followers of Jesus.

When we steadfastly persevere in worshiping in the house of God and in serving in our accustomed places, we will be surprised at what happens. The light and joy of faith will again become real. The assurance of God's presence will once more bless our lives.

Third, prayer is enriched when it is shared with other seekers. Paul challenged his readers to strive "together" with him. The strength of prayer is multiplied when we join a group of friends in sharing the experience of seeking God.

Fourth, there is power in intercessory prayer. Paul asks that petitions be directed to God for him. Christ invites us to take to the heavenly Father all the needs of our personal lives and of our world. God's answer awaits the earnest prayers of those who seek him.

Prayer is available to every follower of Jesus. Its power increases as the discipline becomes more firmly fixed in our daily lives.

PRAYER

Keep alive within us, O God, the desire to know and serve thee. Stir us to new dedication in prayer. Help us each day to seek thy presence. In Jesus' name. *Amen.*

Read Ps. 116

4th Day

GOD'S NATURE GIVES HOPE TO PRAYER

> *Let us therefore come boldly unto the throne of grace, that we may obtain mercy, and find grace to help in time of need.*
>
> —HEB. 4:16

At first thought it would appear a sign of human arrogance to suggest that we "come boldly unto the throne of grace." Such an approach would seem an affront to God. We cannot understand what the words mean unless we understand the mission of Jesus.

Jesus made it clear that God understands human nature. He knows that a certain man has lived a sheltered life. The quiet virtue which prevailed in his home made a lasting influence upon his character. Another man has a temperament which is not easily controlled. His passions flame easily into action. The individual first mentioned may find it easy to live a good life; he may fail to understand the weakness of the other. Often men condemn what they do

69

not understand. In the experience of Christ God had plumbed the depths of our humanity. He understands the struggles of the soul.

John C. Fremont deserves a place on any list of outstanding Americans. He was an eminent explorer, a general in the Mexican War, a candidate for the vice-presidency of his country. In common with many of us he was subject to periods of depression when his life and work seemed meaningless. While exploring in the Rockies he faced one such experience. He wrote a letter to his wife which included this sentence: "If only we could live forever on the heights, the fear and uncertainty would vanish, and we would be as kings."

Many of us have experienced moments when we would agree with John C. Fremont. The psychologists have a term which they use to describe this mental attitude. They call it the law of alternation. It means that we have some days or weeks when we are buoyant in spirit, but others when we feel discouraged and defeated.

These changes in personality cannot be entirely eliminated. They have a physical basis within the human glands. Even the most devout mystics were subject to certain moments when God seemed far removed from human affairs.

We cannot avoid the low hours, but we can limit the depth of depression which they bring and the length of time which they remain to bother us. When we keep close to God and utilize the resources which he makes available, we learn how to overcome such handicaps.

This foundation of faith encourages us to seek God through the avenue of prayer. We are privileged to "come boldly to the throne of grace." Through our seeking we find "grace to help in time of need."

PRAYER

Dear Father, we lift our hearts to thee in prayer. With confident hope we seek thy presence. We walk the path which Jesus has blazed. Let thy grace be sufficient in this our hour of need. In Jesus' name. *Amen.*

Read Heb. 4:12-16

5th Day

GOD'S SECRET OF PRAYER

> *The Spirit also helpeth our infirmities: for we know not what we should pray for as we ought.*
>
> —ROM. 8:26

Jesus reminds us that because of our weaknesses we do not know what to pray for, but that the spirit of God helps and guides us. Someone has said that "prayer is the Divine within us appealing to the Divine above us."

Two human factors make it difficult for us to be wise in our prayers. First, we are unable to foresee the future. Our vision cannot penetrate a year or even a day. We may pray for something which will bring harm to us and to others because we cannot see ahead. Second, we cannot pray aright because we do not understand what will be best for us. We are often like a child who wants something which his mother knows will not be good for him. Then God, like the mother, must make the decision which he knows will be wise.

A current novel deals with the life of Cortez, the famous explorer. The author describes him as a man of sensitive nature. Greater than his drive to find gold was his desire to know more about God. He wrote in his diary: "In my best moments I perceive that God is the Perfection to which my soul must aspire if my life is to have any meaning."

In our better moments we are aware that we must live according to God's will. We are uncomfortable when our days are swallowed up in empty struggle.

Awareness of God slips out of our minds when we fail to seek his presence. When we substitute the daily newspaper for the Bible we sink to the newspaper level of thinking. When our stewardship of material possessions is forgotten in a never-ending battle to gain more luxuries for ourselves and our families we sink to the level where things seem the highest value in life.

Regular practice of the discipline of prayer makes room for faith in God. We learn to measure the values of daily living by divine standards. And best of all, we receive the strength which God freely offers to those who seek him. Cortez was speaking for men and women in our day when he declared that God is the goal "to which my soul must aspire if my life is to have any meaning."

Greek religion was filled with these insights. Pythagoras

commanded his followers not to pray for themselves because they could never in their ignorance know what was wise for them. Socrates taught his pupils to pray for the good things, but not to list them, for God would decide what was wise.

None of us are acquainted with our real needs. We cannot with our limited understanding grasp the total plan of the eternal. It is enough for us to bring our needs to God, allowing his spirit to interpret for us.

The power which is available through prayer is often lost when we assume the attitude of a commander who is summoning God to satisfy his personal desires. The best approach to prayer is that of Jesus: "Father, into Thy hands I commend my spirit."

PRAYER

We thank thee, O God, that we are made to know thee and to do thy will. Help us to follow those disciplines which will make thy presence a daily joy, and the doing of thy will a daily satisfaction. In Jesus' name. *Amen.*

Read Ps. 84:1-12

WHEN WE PRAY FOR OTHERS

Pray for us.

—I Thess. 5:25

It is a Christian privilege to pray each day for family and friends. Followers of Jesus are called upon to remember in prayer all who are entrusted with leadership and authority. It is a Christian obligation to pray for those carrying heavy loads and for those who have drifted away from God.

What difference does it make if we pray for people? The answer to this question depends upon our understanding of how God works through prayer.

In the first place, God is able to do more than he could have done without our prayers. We understand this principle of faith if we recall an occasion when we were strengthened and encouraged because we knew family or friends were praying for us. We felt new power. We had courage to face the necessary hardships. God was able to do more for us than would have been possible if someone had not prayed for our health and guidance.

Secondly, God is able to change our attitudes through the prayers we make for others. He deepens our concern. He leads us to accept responsibility to help those for whom we pray.

The mayor of Houston, Texas, recently called a meeting of the leaders of agencies which work with youth to discuss the problem of juvenile delinquency. A group of ministers and social workers spent several hours searching for ways to combat the difficult situation. At the conclusion of the meeting the mayor asked a prominent Christian layman to lead the group in prayer. The man astounded those present by saying, "I'm sorry. Please ask someone else to pray." Everyone knew the man to be a devoted Christian. His leadership and gifts had often helped to contribute to a better city. They had heard him pray on many occasions. When the murmurs of unbelief had subsided the man went on: "Every time I pray for a situation in this city which needs correction God always appoints me chairman of the committee to do something about it. I just do not have time and strength to devote to this matter."

God puts it into our hearts to serve him when we make our prayers of intercession. He gives us strength to become his means to answer our petitions.

Thirdly, we bow in humility before the miracle of answered prayer. There is a plus element in prayer which eludes our understanding. God brings forces to bear which are beyond the reach of our finite minds. We give expression to our hopes and longings. Then in faith we wait for God to give the answer. If we recognize that our will may not be his desire and plan we can still worship and adore as the answered prayer takes a different form from what we prayed for. The answer is often in keeping with our petitions, but always we can trust his wisdom and love.

PRAYER

We thank thee, O God, for answered prayer. Help us to be the channel through which the miracles of thy grace may flow to bless the lives of others. Keep us humble lest we want our desires fulfilled more than we want thy will to be done. May our prayers be worthy of the Christ whom we love and serve. In his name. *Amen.*

Read Ps. 82

7th Day

THE HIGHER LEVELS OF PRAYER

> *Blessed be thou, Lord God of Israel our father, for ever and ever.*
>
> —I CHRON. 29:10

Gregory of Nyssa preached a sermon on the Lord's Prayer many centuries ago. This is what he had to say about the goal of prayer:

The effect of prayer is union with God, and if someone is with God, he is separated from the enemy. Prayer is the delight of the joyful as well as the solace of the afflicted. Prayer is intimacy with God and contemplation of the invisible. Prayer is the enjoyment of things present and the substance of things to come.

These words of the early Christian saint suggest several principles which are helpful as we grow in the experience of prayer:

76

1. Prayer unites the human spirit with the spirit of God. Genuine prayer enables us to find our best selves through surrender to the purposes and will of the heavenly Father.

Almost every known religion recognizes the endless struggle which goes on between the will of God and the will of man. Buddhism strives to annihilate all human desires. Mohammedanism puts the destiny of man at the will of Allah. Christianity, on the other hand, regards the human soul as the greatest of God's creations. When we come closest in fellowship with the divine we do not lose our identity as persons, but we rediscover our best selves. Prayer enables us to achieve ever more worthy goals as we merge our purposes with those of Almighty God.

2. Prayer serves in hours of happiness as well as in moments of hardship. The saints experienced their highest moments in prayer when they were contemplating the glory and majesty of God. They had nothing to ask except the privilege of praising God for his goodness.

Any Christian who sets aside regular periods for meditation can witness that petitions are never as numerous when time is spent considering the greatness of God. We discover that many of our desires are already known to him, or that his mercy is already at work.

3. Prayer is fellowship with God. It enables us to understand the forces which are invisible. Insecurity and loneliness are banished. We are conscious that the presence is always near us, the living Christ is close beside us.

Arthur J. Gossip told of the advice he gave a farmer in Scotland who complained that God seemed far away and beyond him. Dr. Gossip suggested that he place an empty chair in front of him and, as he prayed, picture Christ as occupying the chair. He was to talk directly to him, then wait expectantly for Christ to answer.

This approach is a practical way to achieve the goal of the mystics. They sought the living presence of God as he was revealed in Christ. Prayer is at its highest level when the praying Christian shares this privilege.

4. Prayer is a source of power in the present hour and assurance for the years to come. It enables us to understand the heart of God and to find the kind of life which has eternal qualities.

Prayer is a pilgrimage in faith. We catch new vistas of the hidden possibilities of such an adventure when we make it a discipline in our daily lives.

PRAYER

Dear Lord, teach us the deeper meaning of prayer. May our fellowship with thee be real. We praise thee for thy creating goodness. Give us thy blessings according to our needs. In Jesus' name. *Amen.*

Read I Chron. 29:10-19

THE DISCIPLINE
OF TITHING

1st Day

THE FOUNDATION FOR TITHING

Whether we live . . . or die, we are the Lord's.
—ROM. 14:8

The Director of Personnel for the Radio Corporation of America tells of his growing concern about the twisted values which are apparent in many young men whom he interviews for positions: "Most college graduates ask three questions as soon as the conversation begins: What is the salary? How much vacation is allowed? What extra benefits are provided in addition to salary?" He tells of a physics major who included $68 for liquor on a three-day expense sheet when he was flown to Philadelphia for an interview. When asked to explain the item the young man replied: "I thought it would make a good impression to show I could handle my drinks."

This attitude threatens the foundations upon which our society is built. No country will remain strong if its people are more interested in ease and luxury than in character and truth.

Wherever the spirit of Jesus rules over the hearts of men the lasting values are always human and spiritual. Where the name of Christ is unknown, life is cheap. Material things and physical pleasures are regarded as supreme. Only as we see through the eyes of the Master do we understand how poor a substitute for life at its best are those drives which send us out in pursuit of things.

The teachings of Jesus include many references to money. He was unconcerned about having money for himself; his interest was in the souls of men. He knew that money and pleasure stand in the way of God's will. He said: "If ye have not been faithful in the unrighteous mammon [money], who will commit to your trust the true riches?" He pleaded with his followers to be faithful stewards of the treasures which his father had entrusted to them. He wanted them to use their money wisely because nothing else in life would be right if that important element were neglected.

Some people argue that the limited references to tithing in the teachings of Jesus indicate that he did not believe in tithing. We lose sight of the fact that he assumed his followers would tithe. "These [tithing] you ought to have done," he said to the Pharisee, "and not to leave the other undone."

All of life was sacred to Jesus. He pleaded with his followers to regard all material things and physical pleasures as holy, but he knew that right attitudes must begin with money.

The recognition of our stewardship through tithing challenges us to assume sacred responsibilities, but it offers also a reason for encouragement. Life has new meaning when we realize that our money is a sacred trust.

PRAYER

Dear Father, we thank thee for life. We thank thee for days to serve thee, and for strength to do thy will. Help us always to be faithful. In Jesus' name. *Amen.*

Read Rom. 14:7-9

2nd Day

TITHING AS A SYMBOL
OF COMPLETE DEDICATION

> *Be content with such things as ye have: for he hath said, I will never leave thee, nor forsake thee.*
>
> —HEB. 13:5

A family escaped before advancing armies in the last war. They had lived in a large house furnished with all that wealth could buy. Early one morning they were warned that enemy soldiers would take possession of their city within an hour. They hastily filled sacks with their most precious possessions. Each member of the family carried on his back all that his strength would bear. When they were forced to leave the road and take to the rough country their burden became too great. They began casting aside silver dishes and expensive pottery. As the pursuing troops came closer they dropped more and more treasures by the way. When at last they escaped to freedom they had discarded all that at first had seemed necessary if they were to live. They found that the most precious thing in the world is life itself.

God is the source of life. Because he entrusted us with this gift, faithful Christians regard life as a sacred trust. We examine our motives to determine whether we are using what we have faithfully and well.

The leaders of the people in Old Testament times were wise in their understanding of human nature. They knew that money and material possessions were held tenaciously at a time when prayers were gladly offered. The people were happy to form religious processions and gather around altars for worship if their wealth was not affected. When the custom of tithing was established it went directly to the root of worship. No act of praise was sincere unless man was willing to include his material possessions in the act of surrender.

Tithing is no less practical and necessary in the twentieth century. Many of us find it easy to worship God if our material possessions are not disturbed. We are willing to surrender our lives to God, but we reserve the right to claim money as our own. Tithing sets a minimum of 10 per cent as the amount of our worldly possessions which we offer to God in return for his gift of life.

Someone told about a man who loudly criticized the principle of tithing. He boasted that he looked upon all of life as a trust and all his money as a gift of God. The financial secretary of his church remarked to the minister: "All his money may be a sacred trust, but God would be much bettter off if he had a tithe."

We need the discipline of tithing. It is not the end of our giving, but it is the historical and practical place to begin. Our worship will take on added meaning when we tithe.

PRAYER

Dear father, we thank thee for life. Thy goodness is the source of all we possess. Help us to be faithful to our trust. Save us from the temptation to offer thee everything except our money. Give us courage to tithe. Thus may our worship be worthy of thy love. In Jesus' name. *Amen.*

Read Prov. 11:1-6

3rd Day

CONQUERING THE LOVE OF MONEY

The love of money is the root of all evil.
—I TIM. 6:10

The life of a prominent businessman was blighted by a consuming desire for money. He knew many moments of material success, and almost as many setbacks, but always he pursued wealth with ceaseless abandon. His father had dreamed that he might serve humanity in the law profession. During his last illness, with his dying breath, his father cried: "Oh, if only my son had not gone after strange gods."

The god of money is not a stranger in this generation. Many men worship the golden image. Their lives are laid at its altar. They scheme and struggle to gain material things. Their first waking thought in the morning, and their last concern at night is for money.

When we substitute the god of mammon for the eternal Creator we deceive ourselves. God is the source of our material wealth. His creation brought forth the fertile fields, the mineral treasures, the mechanical progress which we claim as our own. Money is only a by-product of the works of the Creator. There would be no money without his providential care.

The word "covetousness" is from a Greek word which means "to want more." Plato described the word as meaning "the accursed love of having." It is an aggressive kind of evil which leads men to pursue their own interests with complete disregard for the rights of others. A Christian writer in the third century describes it as that spirit which leads us to grasp at things which we have no right to take.

Covetousness is the opposite of stewardship. The covetous person regards everything as his own if he can get it; the steward thinks of everything as belonging to God and regards himself as a faithful trustee. When a Christian grows in the discipline of stewardship toward all of life he follows the example of Christ; when a man grows more covetous he develops habits which have power to destroy both himself and others.

Because God is the giver of all we possess, he has the right to expect us to use his treasures with a sense of sacred trust. We should not be surprised by the reminder of the Bible that the Creator's anger and sorrow are stirred by our unfaithfulness. He would not be God if he had no concern with the way we handle his gifts.

A faithful Christian recognizes that God is the source of all he owns. All money and material goods are to be administered wisely and well. As an acknowledgment of our heavenly Father's bountiful provision for all our needs we follow the custom of faithful men in all ages by setting aside at least a tithe to do his work in the world.

PRAYER

We have too often worshiped strange gods, O Lord. Forgive us. Help us this day to acknowledge thy goodness and to use wisely and well all thy gifts. In Jesus' name. *Amen.*

Read I Tim. 6:1-10

4th Day

THE BROADER ADVENTURES OF TITHING

It is more blessed to give than to receive.

—ACTS 20:35

When a Christian begins to tithe we assume that he will set aside 10 per cent of his earnings. Such a standard is a low measure of giving. The Old Testament demanded the tithe as reasonable and necessary for faithful Hebrews. We know that the New Testament brought a higher and nobler understanding of God and of his truth. Too many followers of Christ accept his gift of a salvation, a love, and a power which exceeded that of the Old Testament, but are satisfied with standards of giving which would have brought shame to Old Testament people.

Even the government goes beyond the tithe in its financial planning. When the income tax was establishd by the Congress of the United States, it was assumed that 15 per cent of the income of taxpayers should go to some form of benevolence or charity.

Many men of Christian conviction recognize that they are stewards of all the money which comes into their hands. The constant reminder of the uncertainty of life in the nuclear age has made the storing up of wealth less appealing than in former generations. It has seemed reasonable to inquire whether money will be any protection unless Christ conquers the evil in the hearts of men.

Numerous foundations have been established in the last decades. Christian men place their fortunes in such foundations, allowing others to distribute wisely the funds which are available for religious or educational purposes.

A. A. Hyde was once asked whether he had gained or lost by his broader adventures in giving. He answered quietly, almost timidly:

Well, for one thing, I've lost the chance to give a million or two to my children, or to somebody else, but it may be that

I have helped them far more than I have hindered them. I have known not a few men who have cursed their descendants for generations by large inheritances. On the other hand, I have won the supreme satisfaction of easing the burdens that were crippling the lives of men. I cannot escape the conviction that a Christian's first duty is to devote his possessions to the promotion of the Kingdom of God. I have merely done my duty as I have seen it.

Tithing is the place to start the experience of giving. This spiritual and practical discipline requires that all we earn will be held in sacred trust. Out of our abundance we will give as we have been blessed.

PRAYER

Dear Father, we thank thee for money. Help us to hold as a sacred trust, not only what we earn, but our ability to earn it. Inscribe in our hearts the assurance that it is more blessed to give than to receive. May our stewardship be worthy of thy gifts. In Jesus' name. *Amen.*

Read Acts 20:28-35

TITHING AND HUMAN NEED

Let us consider one another to provoke unto love and to good works.

—HEB. 10:24

In a community in Iowa a displaced family has won admiration by their eagerness to be good citizens and by the witness of their lives to the faith which is in them. One day the father announced that he was sending his overcoat to his brother in Poland. Someone inquired whether he himself did not need the coat in that cold climate. "I have a sheepskin jacket," he replied, "which I can wear to work. I only need an overcoat when I go to church. I will be cold only a few times each week, but my brother is cold all the time."

Christians are encouraged by the writer of Hebrews to "consider one another." That is, we are to be aware of the joys and sorrows of those about us. When the body of an aged woman was found in a rooming house in Chicago the physician who signed the death certificate wrote, "slow starvation." She had been dying of hunger for more than a year. Her neighbors later talked about the tragedy. "We never dreamed that she didn't have money enough to buy food," they said. They were too busy to "consider one another."

But the writer of Hebrews goes further. He says that we must be so much aware of the needs of those about us that it will "provoke unto love and to good works." Tithing provides us with the means by which we can respond to human need. The regular practice of this discipline makes possible a fund upon which we can draw at moments when we are confronted with opportunities to help.

Recently I saw a letter from a Korean student who had returned from four years in the United States to work among his own people. He told of having to borrow money so he could pay a large sum in advance for a small tenement where he could live. His meager salary was not sufficient to pay even the exorbitant interest on the loan. He was in dire distress. A layman said quietly that he would give the cash necessary to get the young man out of the clutches of the moneylenders. Several in the group looked at him in surprise, for the sum was large. "Don't give me credit," he said, "the money will come out of my tithing account."

The discipline of tithing provides each one who practices it with a fund through which he is able to "consider one another," and to help when "provoked unto love and to good works." The account will often be depleted, but he then will find courage to go far beyond the tithe to give generously as God has prospered him.

Systematic tithing serves both to increase our sensitivity to the needs of God's children and to provide means by which we can help them.

PRAYER

Kindle our sense of responsibility to those about us, O God. Make us uneasy in the presence of suffering and need. Give us joy as we use our tithe to give help to thy children. May we know that our loving service unto the least of these, our brothers, is rendered unto thee. In Jesus' name. *Amen.*

Read Ps. 123

6th Day

USING THE TITHE WISELY

Seek ye first the kingdom of God.
—MATT. 6:33

The Christian who tithes is wise if he separates the tithe from the rest of his funds. Confusion and loss of satisfaction result when the tithe is paid out of a checking account as one of many monthly bills. Some tithers have set up a separate banking account for their tithe money; others use a metal box into which they place their tithe when wage or salary is received. Whenever tithe money is set aside a Christian is saying, "This is the Lord's. It's his money." When he follows this disipline he acknowledges that God is the source of all life. Such an admission is important. It is the foundation of all vital faith.

Many questions arise when consideration is given to how the tithe shall be used. There are no simple rules to guide us. Many sincere Christians are in disagreement as to what the Bible teaches. As is true with many experiences in Christian living, it is necessary to couple the admission that the money is God's with a prayerful desire to be guided by his spirit. Divine direction is available for all who seek it.

Certain Christian denominations believe that all of the tithe must be given through the church. One group demands that the tithe be used for missionary service beyond the walls of the local church.

The teachings of Jesus would seem to require a broader interpretation of the causes to which our tithe will be directed. It is well to recall that the spirit of Jesus in men led to the establishment of nearly all the humanitarian and social welfare institutions which serve the modern community. Hospitals came into being because of Christian concern for the sick; orphanages and homes were born out of a desire to help those who were unfortunate. Schools and colleges were established by Christian men who wanted the spirit of Christ to rule over the minds and hearts of growing youth.

It is reasonable, then, to conclude that our tithe may be used in part to support the interests which are related to the kingdom of God in the world. If the Red Cross, the Community Fund, and many other organizations and institutions are doing the work of Christ, it is right and proper that we should help to support them with our tithe.

However, there are many people in every community who are outside the church, and who can and do give to such agencies. So it is reasonable that a large part of our tithe, perhaps 70 to 80 per cent, will go directly into the church.

Jesus said to men when he was on earth, "Seek ye first the kingdom of God." The tithe will be wisely used when we are seeking to further the kingdom of God in the community and in the world.

PRAYER

Dear Father, we give thanks for the privilege of tithing. Thy presence becomes more real when we acknowledge thy goodness by our gifts. Direct us by thy spirit into the Christian use of thy money. Help us to advance thy kingdom by our tithes. In Jesus' name. *Amen.*

Read Matt. 6:24-34

7th Day

THE REWARDS OF TITHING

> *He who sows bountifully will also reap bountifully.*
>
> —II Cor. 9:6 (R.S.V.)

Tithing is a source of personal power for daily living. It not only exacts obligations; it gives rewards. Some of the satisfactions are those which come to any person who shares generously of himself and his means to help others.

Carlyle told of an incident which happened when he was a child. He was alone in the house when a beggar knocked at the door and asked for something to eat. On a boyish impulse he broke into his own savings bank and gave the beggar all that was in it. He wrote that never before or after did he know such sheer, joyous happiness as came to him that day.

There is joy in giving. The psychologist may explain the process as release from feelings of guilt caused by other moments when selfish interest led us to choose unworthy means to gain our desires. The Christian faith needs no such explanation. Christ summarized what would be the experience of his followers in every age when he said: "He that loseth his life . . . shall find it."

Happiness often escapes us when we labor to possess things and money. The gadgets of our modern civilization are no defense against boredom and defeat. When we tithe we tap a lasting source of inner power.

We also discover that the remaining nine tenths of our income often seems to go further than the full ten tenths did formerly. There is a practical explanation for this. Tithing tends to decrease the area of our wants. Because God is real and life is holy, we feel less desire to keep up with the pressure of worldliness around us. Clothes and gadgets are less necessary to happiness. Spiritual values rule our desires.

Again, tithers avoid the stress and strain which comes through pressure to support worthy causes. We have money available to give. The question we face is not how much we can spare of our money, but how much of the Lord's funds should be set aside for this appeal. We are trustees of an account which belongs, not to us, but to God.

Furthermore, tithers feel a sense of comradeship with other men who are helping to make a better world. The money which we invest in the church at home and around the world gives us hope for tomorrow. It relates us definitely to others who share a joyous expectation of the triumph of Christ.

Best of all, tithing opens channels through which the power of God can enter our lives. The tither acknowledges the greatness of God. He is aware of the endless supply of blessings which surround him. He not only has daily fellowship with the heavenly Father, but he allows God to do what he wants to do for all men. His life is open to receive the inflowing of divine power.

PRAYER

We thank thee, O Lord, for the privilege of tithing. It has brought us joy. Thy power has filled our lives as we have acknowledged thy goodness with our gifts. We bow in humility before thy grace. Keep us faithful in our giving. In Jesus' name we pray. *Amen*.

Read II Cor. 9:1-6

THE DISCIPLINE
OF WITNESSING

1st Day

OVERCOMING A HESITANCY TO WITNESS

Ye shall be witnesses unto me.

—ACTS 1:8

"Ye shall be witnesses unto me," said Jesus. He assured his followers that they would receive personal power as they told others the good news of God's love.

It is easy to remain silent about our faith when we are with individuals, or with a group, where Christ is neglected or scorned. We assume that people will be Christians if they are interested. We tell ourselves that the church is close at hand to help those who are eager to find God.

Our hesitancy to share our faith is rebuked when we consider the sacrifices which followers of Jesus have made in every age to tell others the good news. The spread of the gospel has cost a great deal in pain and ridicule.

John Wesley wrote of an incident in the village of Wednesbury when he went there to win converts for Christ:

95

To attempt speaking was vain, for the noise on every side was like the roaring of the sea. So they dragged me along till we came to the town, where, seeing the door of a large house open, I attempted to go in; but a man, catching me by the hair, pulled me back into the middle of the mob. They made no more stop till they had carried me through the main street, from one end of town to the other.

Why did John Wesley endure such abuse? He would be quick to reply to our question by saying: "I must tell men everywhere of Christ the Saviour."

The smoke of a thousand African villages where men and women had never heard of Christ drew David Livingstone like a magnet. He proclaimed the gospel on the dark continent by his life as well as by his words. The natives loved him and gave their hearts to his Christ. His countrymen honored him by bringing his body to Westminster Abbey to be buried. He has no monument—only his name: "David Livingstone." Below it is the verse: "Other sheep I have which are not of this fold; them also I must bring."

When we affirm faith in Christ we enlist in a movement. Our commission to witness is from God. It is an inner compulsion which comes from knowing what it means to be without Christ. Because we have found release from the burden of guilt and a power which makes daily living a continued joy, we want others to have it. Rebuffs and refusals are expected. We know how appealing pleasure can appear to be. But experience tells us that worldly satisfactions are empty when sorrow and trial press upon us. Our courage to witness comes from a desire that others may know the joy which fills our hearts.

The Christian witness is needed in our day. A host of people are trying to live without God. They long to know what it means to be forgiven. Whatever the cost, it is our duty and privilege to share the good news with a needy world.

PRAYER

Bolster our courage, O Lord, that we may become living witnesses of our faith. Make us sensitive to the places and times when we ought to speak out for thee. Save us from the temptation not to care when men are living without a knowledge of thee. In Jesus' name. *Amen.*

Read Acts 1:1-9

2nd Day

A CONCERN FOR SOULS

> *They that have not heard shall understand.*
> —Rom. 15:21

If we know the love of Christ we will want to share it. Our concern will include all kinds of people. We will see hidden possibilities in those whose selfish greed, sordid appetites, and unpleasant habits make us want to shun them. We will want to be used to reach the most hopeless and disagreeable examples of what sin does to life.

T. E. Lawrence was once journeying across the desert

97

with a company of Arabs. For many days the wind had blown the sand in choking clouds. Lawrence and the Arabs held hoods over their faces as they leaned forward against the raging storm. Suddenly someone shouted, "Where is Jasmin? Look, his camel has no rider." A second said: "He killed a Turkish tax collector and fled to the desert. Let him go." A third said, "He is not strong in the head, perhaps he is lost in a mirage; he is not strong in body, perhaps he has fainted and fallen off his camel." The first man replied, "What does it matter? Jasmin is not worth one piece of silver." With that the Arabs turned their camels into the storm and rode on. But Lawrence went back over the trail. After more than an hour of searching he saw something half buried in the drifting sand. It was Jasmin, blind and mad with heat and thirst. Lawrence set him on his camel, gave him his last drops of water, and slowly plodded back to the company. When he came up to them the Arabs looked in amazement. "Here is Jasmin, not worth a piece of silver, saved by our leader at the risk of his life."

Christ's heart burned with a desire to seek and to save those who were lost. He gave his life for their salvation. A man in Dallas, Texas, tells of speaking to a business associate about his need for Christ. He did this many times, yet always met with indifference. Recently a series of special meetings was held in the church where this man is a leader. He invited his friend to attend a service as his guest. The man accepted. As he was leaving the home the man's wife spoke up: "But that's our 'rasslin' night on television," she said. The husband agreed that he could not afford to miss the program. It was frustrating to the witness, but he would not admit defeat. "I'm not through yet," he said. "I'll keep at it. Someday he will recognize his need for Christ."

Christians are committed to tell people everywhere of the one who came to bring new life and hope to those who are living without God. Our witness will be needed while even one man or woman or youth is blind to God's truth. He may seem unlovely and unwanted, or just bewildered by the complex demands of our day. In either case, God cares. He needs us to tell the good news of salvation and faith.

PRAYER

Save us, O God, from spiritual arrogance. Give us courage this day to love people as Christ loved them. Let thy spirit direct our witness that men may find new life in thee. In Jesus' name. *Amen*.

Read John 15:1-10

THE PLACE TO WITNESS
IS WHERE YOU ARE

He was lost, and is found.

—LUKE 15:24

An architect in Florida told of a tragic experience which convinced him that he must witness for Christ every day. He had ignored religion and the church. After a number of years his wife gave birth to a son. Because he wanted the best in life for his child, he joined the church. He attended services almost every Sunday. After four years he accepted an invitation to visit one night a month with other laymen. He had a feeling of satisfaction when people he had called on were taken into the membership. Yet visiting each month remained merely an obligation.

Then came a tragic accident. His six-year-old boy was attacked by a shark while wading in shallow water at a beach near Miami. He rushed in, fought for the life of his son and by a supreme effort dragged him away from the shark. But the boy lost his right arm. He was close to death, and it was many weeks before his recovery was assured.

"I have learned something from this experience," the architect said: "I have learned that a man can't get along without faith. I couldn't have kept going without Christ. The strength which came during these weeks was from God. Now I'm telling everyone I meet about it. I'm witnessing, not just one night a month, but every day. I'm speaking to people in my neighborhood, the men I contact in my business, my friends in the service club. I'm using every opportunity to witness for Christ."

The need of men for the Savior can be seen on every hand. The woman who is anxiously striving for social recognition needs Christ. The man who shows his insecurity by foul language needs Christ. The boy who belongs to a neighborhood gang needs Christ. The girl who scorns virtue needs Christ. The people are on every side. They pretend that they are carefree, but inside they are very insecure. Their resistance to the call of God has made them feel guilty. They push away the yearning for something better, but they cannot escape it. They long to know the Savior. They need the power which only he can give.

Men and women are often waiting for the evidence of our concern. Those to whom we speak may not want to give up their lust, their dishonesty, their pleasure, or their doubts. But a plus element is at work. God is interested. His presence is close at hand to convict and to persuade. Yet he needs your voice and mine. The place for each of us to witness is wherever we are.

The Florida architect demonstrates the teaching of the Bible that witnessing is a source of daily strength. One who tells about Christ wherever he finds needy people receives for himself a gift beyond measure. He has personal power sufficient to meet every test.

PRAYER

Dear Father, we give thanks for thy gift of Christ. We need him if we are to be our best selves. Stir within us a desire to share our faith. Help us to witness wherever we are, not only by our words but by our lives. In Jesus' name. *Amen.*

Read Luke 15:1-24

4th Day

PERSUASIVE WITNESSING

> *My heart's desire and prayer to God is, that they might be saved.*
>
> —ROM. 10:1

Paul did not rage in anger because the Jews of his day failed to recognize the lordship of Jesus. His attitude was one of wistful longing. He pleaded with them to accept the truth of the gospel.

The darkest pages in the history of the Christian church have been those when mistaken followers of Jesus were convinced that force and political power were necessary to convert an unyielding world. The Inquisition will always remind us that cruelties no less fearful than twentieth-century gas chambers and concentration camps were used to compel men to become Christians.

The discipline of witnessing calls for a deep and lasting concern for people. It requires that our "heart's desire" be turned in the direction of leading men to Christ. There is no room for anger because men refuse to respond. There is no place for arrogance and superiority.

In A.D. 496 Christian missionaries arrived at the court of Clovis, king of the Franks. They told the story of the death of Jesus on the cross. The hand of the ruler gripped the hilt of his sword. "If I and my Franks had been there," he said, "we would have stormed Calvary and rescued him from his enemies."

The reaction of the monarch is understandable. We often have felt that, had we been there, we would have found a way to rescue Jesus from those who crucified him.

Yet we were not there, nor can we return to the scene to change the pattern of history. But the selfish greed of the Jewish authorities who plotted against Jesus is still in evidence in our day. The callous indifference of the Roman soldiers is still apparent in a countless host of people who avoid the challenge of Christianity for life in our century.

We are not asked to take up arms to destroy opposition to the faith. Our responsibility is to tell far and wide the story of God's love. Our privilege is to make certain that the death of Christ was not in vain—that godlessness, greed, hatred, and selfishness may be overcome by surrender of life to the will of the Master.

A feeling of urgency about the danger of godlessness in an atomic age tempts us to bitterness against those who refuse to accept the truth of the Christian faith. Our impatience sometimes gives way to resentment; but there is no place for such feelings in the religion of Jesus. The cross is the symbol of our faith. We must be willing to suffer, if necessary, for those we would win.

Witnessing is persuasive and appealing when our heart's desire and prayer is that men may be saved. First their problems must become our problems, their successes our joys, and their sorrows our heartaches. Then when we speak of God's love for them our words are convincing.

PRAYER

Dear Father, help us this day to be persuasive witnesses of thy truth. Save us from the temptation to impatience with those who walk in darkness. May those about us see the spirit of Jesus in all we do. In his name. *Amen.*

Read Rom. 10:1-10

5th Day

SPIRITUAL DARING

> *Watch ye, stand fast in the faith, quit you like men, be strong.*
>
> —I COR. 16:13

George Orwell in *The Prevention of Literature* quoted the words of an old hymn to describe character at its best:

> Dare to be a Daniel,
> Dare to stand alone:

104

Dare to have a purpose firm,
Dare to make it known.

Orwell concludes that most of us in this generation put the word "don't" at the beginning of each line.

It is easier and more comfortable to follow the customs of the crowd. Television, radio, and newspapers use their influence to persuade us to dress alike, to follow similar social customs, and even to think alike. They hammer relentlessly on the theme that attractiveness and popularity require us to use the same soaps, possess the same household appliances, and drink the same beverages.

It is not strange that we should question at times whether the Christian faith has meaning for our generation. We may wonder whether Christ is necessary for life in our day. Even if we are persuaded that faith is important, we may not have the spiritual daring to tell others about it.

The only adequate source of power for witnessing stems from the burning conviction that men must have faith in order to live, that our world is plunging toward destruction unless Christ is made real in millions of hearts.

Rudyard Kipling once observed William Booth as he boarded a ship at an English port. He was escorted by a large company of tambourine-beating representatives of the Salvation Army. The incident was revolting to the dignified Kipling. Later he came to know General Booth and told him how much he disapproved of what he had seen. "Young man," said Booth, "if I thought I could win one more soul for Christ by standing on my hands and beating a tambourine with my feet I would learn to do it."

Whenever a Christian gives witness to his faith there are those who regard him as peculiar. It is natural to look with suspicion upon those who offer something which promises to change lives or to change the world. Many people don't want their lives made different; they resent anything which threatens to change the world that provides them with comfort and pleasure.

Our witness will remain hesitant until we recognize that men are lost without faith. If Christ makes no difference in our daily lives, we can remain complacent while those around us strive for physical satisfactions. But if commitment to Christ marks the dividing line between darkness and light, between time and eternity, we cannot remain silent.

Knowing that surrender to the will of Christ is man's best hope of salvation, we will do anything and go anywhere to win one soul for the Master. That conviction is the explanation for the agelong and world-wide influence of Christianity. If we lose it in our century we will consign humanity to the darkness of a godless night.

PRAYER

Give us a concern for souls, O Lord. By the power of the faith that is in us help us to go out into each new day with an eagerness to share the good news of Christ. In his name, we pray. *Amen.*

Read II Cor. 5:11-19

THE WITNESS OF A GREAT LIFE

That they may see your good works, and glorify your Father which is in heaven.

—MATT. 5:16

The daily lives of those who are surrendered to Christ are often as effective as words to lead men and women to faith. The biographer of Henry M. Stanley wrote about his experience while searching in Africa for David Livingstone. Stanley had boasted that he was an agnostic. When he returned to America the author could say of him: "Stanley now believes in Christ because there is a Livingstone."

Many other men and women trace their decision to become a follower of Jesus to the radiant and dedicated example of someone who had given heart and mind to the Master.

Paul declared that we are living epistles of the gospel. People learn what it means to be a Christian when they observe us. We are witnessing every day by what we do.

A young soldier who had been seriously wounded was brought into a makeshift operating room at an Army hospital. The chaplain was summoned. He spoke words of courage and comfort and accompanied the boy to his bed when the surgeons had finished their work. Nurses and orderlies were busy with other patients, so the chaplain remained at the lad's side throughout the night. He moistened his lips, covered him with extra blankets when he was chilled, and spoke words of encouragement during moments of rationality. Toward morning the young man's eyes opened and he looked intently at the one who had stayed with him. "Chaplain," he said, "you're a Christian." "I try to be," answered the chaplain. "If Christianity makes you do what you have done for me," the youth said, "tell me about it, because I want it."

Men have often accepted the Christian faith because they observed people who were changed by their commitment to Christ. It was so when Paulinus, the eloquent and dedicated missionary, preached the gospel to King Edwin of England. The king called a council which met in the village of York in the year 627. The chief priest of paganism declared that the pagan gods had done nothing for them and that he was willing to try another religion. Then one of the nobles said: "O King, Paulinus is a Christian. He lives as if he had a hope which we do not have. Let us hear him."

The words and the example of Paulinus were enough to persuade those who heard him. The pagan temple was destroyed, and in its place a Christian church was built. York Minster, one of the great cathedrals of Christendom, stands today at that spot. It testifies to the radiant faith of the one who witnessed there.

Christ will be accepted by our neighbors and friends if we demonstrate every day that faith has made us different. The world is waiting to see what faith has done in those who claim Christ as Lord and Savior.

PRAYER

Forgive us, O Lord, for the feeble witness of our daily

lives. Help us to live today in such a way that men will desire to know the Christ whom we serve. *Amen.*

Read Matt. 5:1-12

7th Day

A WITNESS TO THOSE WHO FALTER

> *Look diligently lest any man fail of the grace of God.*
>
> —HEB. 12:15

Two boys were in a hiking party in the rugged mountains of Montana. When evening came they were missing. Somewhere in a wild country they had left the trail to examine a rock or a flower, and now they were lost. Their father raised an alarm. Scores of men fanned out over that vast wilderness. The father ran back over the trail shouting continually in the hope that the boys might hear his voice. The search went on through the night and all the next day until at last they were found, tired and hungry, but unharmed.

Many Christians wander from the way of Christ. Sometimes worldly interest captures their attention. They forsake Christian practices to indulge in physical satisfactions. They do not mean to renounce Christ; they merely stray away. They were sincere when they accepted him as their Savior and Lord and when they promised loyalty to his church. With the passing years they frequently saw position and wealth within their reach. They knew they would be forced to renounce Christian ideals if they were to get what they wanted. They made the choice and left the way of Christ.

Sometimes fading loyalty is reflected in failure to attend church. Often it is seen in a denial of our obligation to support the church with our efforts and our gifts. Always it is marked by a disregard of prayer and Bible reading.

A recent survey by a major denomination revealed the fact that 35 per cent of all church members never attend church; 45 per cent never give their money; 48 per cent never pray; 55 per cent never read the Bible; 74 per cent never have family devotions.

Someone has said that the greatest untapped resource of the church is to be found among the members who fail to be loyal to Christ. They could build new churches and send missionaries into foreign lands; they could remove every need for additional teachers and leaders; they could change the social habits of the nation—miracles could happen if they were controlled by the spirit of Christ.

In one of his essays Meister Eckhart remarked that there are always some who will follow Christ halfway, but there are not many who will follow him the other half. This is the tragedy of our day.

One mark of unfaithfulness is the loss of personal power. Careless followers of Jesus could live victoriously, but instead they are beset by anxieties and fears. They have turned away from God's endless source of inner strength.

If we believe in Jesus we must be concerned for all who

are indifferent. It is our duty to plead and to strive unceasingly until every wanderer has returned.

PRAYER

Dear Father, we bow before the mystery of thy love for each one of us. Help us to strive to find all those who have wandered away. Kindle our concern for every person, remembering that they, too, are precious in thy sight. In Jesus' name. *Amen.*

Read Ps. 67

THE DISCIPLINE
OF SERVICE

1st Day

THE GLORY OF SERVICE

> *Glory, honour, and peace, to every man that*
> *worketh good.*
>
> —ROM. 2:10

We believe in the God who was revealed in Christ. Our
convictions make us want to serve others in his name. We
recognize an obligation to use our strength and means to
help those who are in need.

Turgenev tells of being stopped on the street by a beggar.
Reaching into his pocket for a coin he discovered that he
had brought no money with him. Impulsively he stretched
out his hand. "My brother," he said, "I can give you nothing but this." The beggar was deeply moved. "You called
me brother," he said, "you took my hand; that, too, is a
gift."

It is always tempting to discharge our duty to people
in need by making a donation. Money is the easiest way
to fulfill our obligation to aid those who are less fortunate.
But the Christian ideal of service requires more of sacrifice
than can be purchased with money alone. Service involves

112

self. It calls for the exercise of sympathy, which in turn places a demand upon our time and efforts.

Financial gifts help to solve many of the problems of those who are in distress, but money does not provide understanding and love. The world is an impersonal and cold battleground for jobless, hungry, or lonely men and women. They need the loving heart of Christ as evidenced in those who claim him as their lord.

Alice Freeman Palmer is remembered as a woman who turned from the pleasures of social life and the comforts of a luxurious home to work with underprivileged girls in the slums of Boston, Massachusetts. She pioneered in gathering together girls who worked in sweatshops or who wandered the streets. She showed them how to care for themselves, how to be good housekeepers, how to live happily with small possessions. One girl was an orphan who had been left to care for a baby brother when her father deserted the family and her mother died. Neighbors in the block where she lived recognized that she possessed a quiet happiness even when her days were spent in a bleak garret room.

After the death of Mrs. Palmer a newspaperman went into the slums to get a story about her work. Someone referred him to the orphan girl. When he asked what Mrs. Palmer had done for her, the girl replied: "She taught me how to live for others. I know now what love really means."

The Christian faith encourages the followers of Jesus to serve needy humanity in his name. Material possessions can help lift the burden from the poor and needy; love can supply the joy which no amount of wealth can buy.

Paul believed that faith must be confirmed by good works. No other attitude is sufficient to satisfy our obligations to God, and to the world.

PRAYER

Strengthen our faith, O God. Give us the awareness that faith must result in acts of service. Save us from blindness to the needs of others and the arrogance which allows us to believe in thee without serving thy cause. In Jesus' name. *Amen.*

Read Rom. 2:1-11

2nd Day

LIVING ACCORDING TO THE TEACHINGS OF JESUS

See that ye refuse not him that speaketh.
—Heb. 12:25

The early Christians did not at first see the importance of the teachings of Jesus. The Crucifixion was looked upon as the act of God by which men were reconciled to him. They gladly shared the glorious news of Christ's resurrection. They were strengthened every day by the assurance of his presence in the Holy Spirit. But they were slow to recognize the significance of his teachings.

The words of Jesus are an essential part of God's revelation of himself in Christ. Jesus not only revealed the heart of his Father; his teachings were the voice of the Father. He used familiar events and experiences to translate God's truth into a language which could be understood by men and women in every age.

Throughout the centuries there have been many periods when Christians ignored the teachings of Jesus. Influential religious bodies have extended their influence with only a passing recognition of the words which Jesus spoke. The church which was established in Rome centered its attention on a ceremonial which makes no reference to the teachings of Jesus. Its code of behavior for believers was formulated by councils or by the head of the church. When new authoritarian laws are necessary, the source is not the teaching of Jesus in the Gospels, but the encyclicals of previous heads of the church.

Many other religious groups have looked to doctrines and dogmas for their authority. It has always been more comfortable—and less dangerous—to ignore the demands of Jesus for love and service.

It is difficult for us to recapture the excitement which was stirred at the turn of the last century when Charles Sheldon's *In His Steps* was published. It appeared originally in serial form in a magazine. When it was reprinted as a book it was eagerly read by a host of Christians. More than six-and-a-half million copies were sold in a generation.

The theme of the book is simple. It raises the question of what would happen in a home, a community, and the world if the followers of Jesus were to follow in his steps, controlled daily by his example and his teachings. It dramatizes the manner in which hate would be banished; people would learn how to forgive one another; loving service would be the mark of a Christian's faith.

Followers of Jesus in every age have discovered a key to vital personal power in the teachings of Jesus. His words are truth; his instructions are law. As we walk every day with him and follow his teachings, we find joy in serving others and power for each day's needs.

PRAYER

Dear Father, help us to walk this day with the Master. Tune our ears to hear him speak. Give us courage to accept and follow his teachings. *Amen.*

Read Heb. 12:25-28

3rd Day

THE MAJESTY OF A DEDICATED LIFE

I am among you as one who serves.

—LUKE 22:27 (R.S.V.)

It is tempting to dwell upon the majesty of Jesus. We often refer to him as "seated on the right hand of God." Even when he walked among the humble people of Galilee there was a kingliness about him which was apparent to those who knew him. Yet Jesus never regarded majesty as something which his father had conferred upon him. He said: "I am among you as one who serves."

Robert Louis Stevenson went to the island of Samoa when he was a victim of tuberculosis. His depleted strength was sapped when he built a small hut which was to be his future home. One evening he lay exhausted on a mat in a corner of the room. He had made no provision for food. Suddenly a native boy appeared bearing a tray on which were a cup of coffee and a roll. Mr. Stevenson said to the boy in the native language: "Great is your forethought." The lad corrected him, saying: "Great is the love."

Jesus fed the hungry multitude, healed the sick, and met the needs of outcasts because of his great love for men. He showed us both the heart of the heavenly Father and the attitude which he expected his followers to take.

History includes many incidents when Christians put service to others above their personal comforts. Their example has sometimes brought ridicule, but it always inspires admiration.

The town of Salem, Massachusetts, was shaken more than a century ago by the discovery that an Italian sailor, in port with a freighter, was a victim of leprosy. After hasty consultation the town fathers decided to place him in isolation on an abandoned farm about twenty miles from the town. In the following months other foreign ships brought more victims of the dread disease. They, too, were sent to the farm, until the colony numbered twenty-three. A young physician named Dr. Charles Parker cared for them. As the number of lepers increased, the anxiety in Massachusetts became a form of hysteria. Pressure was brought on the legislature to take action. A law was enacted banishing the lepers to an uninhabited island far offshore. Then the question arose as to who would care for these sick and dying men. Dr. Parker announced that he would give up his medical practice and go to live on the island. "Why? Why?" he was asked again and again. "I'm a Christian," he replied simply. "How can I do less than what I know to be right?" He left his wife and children and ministered to the lepers for three years, until at last the survivors were moved to the leprosarium in Carville, Louisiana.

When we affirm our belief in Christ we enlist on his side in the struggle against poverty, hunger, and pain. We, too, should be able to say, "I am among you as one who serves."

PRAYER

Dear Father, keep us from the temptation to strive for the rewards of the world. Help us to find our rest in thee and our purpose in the example of the Christ who came among us as one who serves. In his name we make our prayer. *Amen.*

Read Prov. 3:11-14

THE TRUE TEST OF FAITH

I am crucified with Christ.

—GAL. 2:20

One of the most severe periods of persecution in Christian history occurred during the reign of the emperor Diocletian. Thousands of faithful men and women were burned at the stake or fed to wild beasts in the arena. Afterwards a question was asked again and again of those who escaped the torture: "Did you deny Christ to save your life?"

Men were aware that cowardice in the face of trial had weakened the faith. The bravery and dauntless courage of those who gave their all had won the reluctant admiration of even the enemies of the church. Many who formerly had been hesitant to be counted as Christians were led to give him their allegiance. On the other hand, those who denied Christ to escape death seemed to give evidence that the faith was merely a foreign cult.

The carelessness of some who profess faith in him is still the chief barrier to the world-wide triumph of Christ. Critics are quick to observe habits of living which are out of keeping with the teachings of Jesus. They smile in superiority when they note dishonesty or lack of reverence in those who are members of the church. They turn away from professing Christians who find convenient excuses to avoid obligations which demand sacrifice.

The apostle Paul could say, "I am crucified with Christ." He suffered imprisonments, stonings, beatings. Someone has said that if Paul were to walk backwards toward the gates of heaven he would be recognized by the stripes on his back.

The hardships which are demanded of us are of a different kind. We are called upon to take a stand for Christ when the people around us are endeavoring merely to satisfy their physical appetites. We are summoned to honesty in worldly affairs, even when honesty is a costly choice. We are compelled to serve others, even when service demands great sacrifice.

In *The Hunchback of Notre Dame* Victor Hugo paints an unforgettable picture of the pitiful Quasimodo. Ugly, misshapen, simple-minded Quasimodo is the symbol of all the pathetic people in our world. The hunchback is dragged into the square, charged with an imaginary offense. He is beaten, and beaten again, and again, while lashed to a stake. As he lies under the hot sun close to unconsciousness a servant girl, Esmeralda, slips out of the jeering crowd to bring him a gourd of water. She puts it to his lips while scornful laughter rings in her ears. When she leaves him Quasimodo looks about him with wonder: "She gave me water! She gave me water!" he whispers.

When confronted with tragic, pitiable humanity we can do no less than offer the best we have in service. Whatever the cost, whatever the sacrifice, we are obligated to help others as God gives us strength. The cross of Jesus means nothing if it does not call us to deeds of service in his name.

PRAYER

Save us, O God, from the temptation to yield to the pressures of the world. Help us to express our gratitude for the

Cross by deeds of self-sacrifice. May Christ have no reason this day to be ashamed of us. In his name we pray. *Amen.*

Read Gal. 2:1-20

5th Day

DEDICATED HANDS AND FEET

> *Wherefore, lift up the hands . . . and make straight paths for your feet.*
>
> —Heb. 12:12

Those who profess faith in Christ are encouraged by the writer of Hebrews to "lift up" their idle hands. That is, we are urged to undertake deeds of service. It may seem strange that the command was not to pray or to read the Bible. The one who was giving guidance for the Christian life believed that fellowship with Christ is more vital and real when each day we are using our hands to help others.

A minister in Arizona told me that his father died when he was a child. His mother was left with two small boys. She accepted every available type of work to earn enough money to buy the simplest necessities of life. She went into homes to work by the day; she took in washing; she sewed long after everyone else was asleep.

"My mother died when I was nine years old," he said. "She never had her picture taken, and I cannot remember how she looked. I can't recall her face at all. But this is the extraordinary thing. I can see her hands plainly, the hands which made such sacrifices for my brother and for me. I can't recall her face, but I remember her hands."

The writer of Hebrews was on firm ground when he urged followers of Jesus to "lift up the hands." The discipline of service enables us to follow the example of our Master.

When we are asked to "make straight paths for our feet," it is a summons to walk uprightly, to live honestly, and to do justly. Noble living is required of every Christian.

A businessman who had the respect of his community was admired for his generosity and friendliness. Then one day I received a letter from a distant city asking if I could find financial help for an elderly woman who was in great need. She proved to be the mother of this business-man. Mother and son had quarreled twenty years before, and he had refused to recognize any further obligation to provide for her support. All confidence in the man's integrity vanished at that moment, for he had rejected the simplest obligation of one who claims to be a Christian.

Our spiritual life cannot be separated from the rest of our interests. We are expected to let the work of our hands and feet be a witness to our faith.

PRAYER

Let our hands, O Lord, be used for thee. May our feet walk in thy paths. By our service may we be counted worthy to receive thy greater gifts. In Jesus' name. *Amen.*

Read Heb. 12:12-15

THE CHALLENGE OF THE BEST

> *Wherefore, my dearly beloved, flee from idolatry.*
>
> —I Cor. 10:14

The statue of Christ by Thorwaldsen is one of the most beautiful and impressive in all the world of art. Thousands of visitors go each year to the church in Copenhagen where it is the center of worship. They look with wonder at the manner in which the artist has captured in stone the spirit of the master. After he had finished his great work Thorwaldsen was offered a commission to carve a likeness of Venus for the Louvre. He answered: "The hand that carved the figure of Christ can never carve the form of a heathen goddess."

To know Christ and to claim him as the lord of life makes it impossible for us to indulge our bodies and minds in that which destroys all that is holy. However attractive social pleasures and material satisfactions may be, we are gripped by a higher loyalty. We are compelled to turn away from evil.

The apostle Paul was aware that the early Christians would be tempted. He counseled them to shun everything which had to do with idols. His advice is no less important in our day. The best way to avoid entanglement with evil is to take a definite stand on the side of that which is right.

The idols of the twentieth century are not made of wood or stone, but we know they exist. How tragic it is when the good life of a nation is undermined because her people

123

worship pleasure or material things. These should remain our servants instead of becoming our gods.

A moving story is told of a grandmother who is bringing up her son's child, for his parents have been killed in an accident. She believed in goodness, and never overlooked an opportunity to instruct the growing boy. As he cracked nuts before the fireplace she would say,

Now, lad, learn this little rhyme by heart while you work:

> Count that day lost
>   Whose low descending sun
> Sees from thy hand
>   No worthy action done.

The boy would repeat the words after her until he had committed them to memory.

We live in a day when many of us regard leisure time as an invitation to relax. We argue persuasively that the pressure of our machine age makes it necessary to "let go" by doing nothing.

The deepest satisfactions of daily living are realized when we use each passing hour with an awareness that our time is a sacred trust.

A certain man was janitor of a village church in New Hampshire for forty-four years. He received no pay for his work, but the church was always spotless. No cold Sunday morning failed to find him at the furnace long before dawn. He welcomed every activity which was planned by any organization, disregarding the extra work it made. Someone asked him why he did it. "This is my life," he replied; "it's my hunting and my fishing, my lodge and my club." Others could say that it was his source of power, for he had a radiance about him which enriched the lives of all he met.

God will release power for our use when we accept joyfully the privilege of helping others. Christ has promised it; experience has proved his promises are sure.

PRAYER

Dear Father, help us to use wisely the days and the hours. Save us from the temptation to waste the treasures thou hast entrusted to us. May we be worthy of thy gifts of power as we serve others in the spirit of Christ. In Jesus' name. *Amen.*

Read Ps. 119:73-80

7th Day

THE GOAL OF LIVING

> *Let us run with patience the race that is set before us.*
>
> —HEB. 12:1

Life in our day is often described as "a rat race." Many people are running in circles, pursued by the pressure to keep up with the crowd. Existence is like a merry-go-round which may be fun while it lasts but is going nowhere.

The Christian life is different. It is a race—but a race toward a goal. Those who profess faith in Christ are on a path which leads toward the kingdom.

When we are summoned to run with "patience" the race of life, the word does not mean quiet renunciation. It refers more to endurance, determination, and steadfast courage. It does not mean a patience which is satisfied to wait indefinitely; nor does it refer to the resigned patience which sits down and decides that nothing can be done. It means the calm persistence which conquers obstacles and overcomes hardships. Such a quality is not spectacular; often the results come from steady plodding toward the goal. It demands that we go onward with determination, facing and surmounting difficulties—never frantic or anxious. Patience will never permit a halt, whatever may be the weariness which tempts us to be discouraged, or the opposition which threatens defeat.

A newspaper cartoon shows two men on Mars looking down at people on the earth as they hurry about, here, there and everywhere. One said, "What are they doing?" The other replied, "They are going." "But," said the first man, "where are they going?" "Oh," the other answered, "They are not going anywhere, they are just going."

Too much of life is aimless. We struggle to get through the twenty-four hours of a day, or the seven days of a week. When it is over we are aware that we have been busy. Our activities have been hectic, but they leave us with a feeling of emptiness. Often we cannot escape the conviction that life is a mad rush that is going nowhere.

The Christian way is different. It makes for dissatisfaction with wasted days and hours. It leads us to examine our purposes and goals. It makes us want to serve as Jesus served; it makes us want to love as Jesus loved. It calls for patient and constant devotion to those practices of loving service which bring the kingdom closer to realization. *Read Rom 12:9*

The efforts which we expend helping people will last long after our striving for money and pleasure has been forgotten. Daniel Webster, in one of his speeches, said:

If we work with marble, it will perish. If we work with brass, time will efface it. If we raise temples, they will crumble into dust. But if we work with immortal souls, we grave on those tablets something which will brighten all eternity.

The lasting mark of our efforts will be left not only on those we serve; we ourselves will find new meaning in daily living. We will run the race of life with strength and finish our course with the assurance of victory.

PRAYER

Dear Father, strengthen our determination to use wisely all thy gifts. Give us the satisfaction of knowing that we are doing thy will. Help us to love as Jesus loved and to serve as Jesus served. In his name we make our prayer. *Amen.*

Read II Cor. 10:1-7